Theology Today
12 The Theology of the Word of God

D1153774

Nihil Obstat:
Jeremiah J. O'Sullivan, D.D.
Censor deputatus
17th September 1970

Imprimatur:
† Cornelius Ep. Corcag. & Ross
29th September 1970

SBN 85342 230 3

Dedication:
To my mother, my 'first preacher',
and to the people of the parish of the
Sacred Heart, Edinburgh, who supported me
in more senses than one whilst this book
was being written.

Theology Today

GENERAL EDITOR:

EDWARD YARNOLD, S.J.

No. 12

The Theology of the Word of God

BY

ALOYSIUS CHURCH, S.J.

FIDES PUBLISHERS INC.

NOTRE DAME, INDIANA

ACKNOWLEDGEMENTS

The Scripture quotations in this publication are from the Revised Standard Version of the Bible, copyrighted 1946 and 1952 by the Division of Christian Education of the National Council of the Churches of Christ in the U.S.A. and used by kind permission. Quotations from The Documents of Vatican II (ed. W. M. Abbott, S.J.) are printed by kind permission of The America Press and Geoffrey Chapman Ltd., London.

Note: as the documents of the Second Vatican Council are frequently quoted in the text, the following abbreviations have been used to save repetition of the longer titles:

Church: Dogmatic Constitution on the Church
Revelation: Dogmatic Constitution on Divine Revelation
Liturgy: Constitution on the Sacred Liturgy
Bishops: Decree on the Bishops' Pastoral Office in the Church
Priestly Formation: Decree on Priestly Formation
Laity: Decree on the Apostolate of the Laity
Ministry of Priests: Decree on the Ministry and Life of Priests
Missions: Decree on the Church's Missionary Activity

CONTENTS

PREFACE

There is an exciting temptation in theology to take a word which is used in several partly different senses and speak as if the senses were identical. For example, the term 'Christ's body' has at least three meanings: his body of flesh and blood, his eucharistic presence and the Church. The three meanings largely coincide, so that St Paul can jump from one sense to another: our bodies belong to Christ's body, therefore we must not put them to unchaste use (1 Cor 6.15-20); we share Christ's eucharistic body, therefore we are united as a single body (1 Cor 10.16-17). But the meanings are not completely interchangeable: thus, the physical properties (weight, colour, etc.) of Christ's natural body are evidently not present in the Eucharist.

There is a similar overlap in the use of the term 'the word'. It can refer to God's revelation and command; but also to the Second Person of the Trinity, the Word made flesh. The preacher tries to put before his listeners God's Word, not only in the first sense, but also in the second. In preaching God's message, he is confronting them with Christ. The identity of the two senses of 'word' is even more complete than that of various senses of 'body'. The Word is present in the word; Christ is present in the Mass not only in the eucharistic species, but also in the readings and the homily.

Fr Church draws on the documents of Vatican II and modern catechetical writings to examine this presence of the Word in the word.

E. J. Yarnold, S.J.

CHAPTER I

THE WORD IN CATHOLIC LIFE

The theme of this book touches closely the day-to-day life of the ordinary Catholic lay-person. This needs saying. For it is not likely, were he asked to talk about the things that affect him closely as a Catholic, that the phrase 'word of God' would spring spontaneously to his lips. Grace, yes; sacraments, yes; obey the Pope, yes; keep the commandments, yes. Only rarely would we get the reply: I am a Catholic because I am one who hears the word of God and tries to keep it.

And yet, our Lord described his true brethren in this way. One day when he was preaching, he was told: 'Your mother and your brethren are standing outside, desiring to see you' (Lk 8.20); and he replied: 'My mother and my brethren are those who hear the word of God and do it' (ibid.). He uses other expressions too, but this sums them up. Indeed, our Lady, symbol of the Church, and model of her members, was the one who said: 'Behold I am the handmaid of the Lord; let it be to me according to your word' (Lk 1.38).

'Let it be to me according to your word'. An apt description of the whole of Christian life? Yes, but one easily open to misunderstanding. 'Your word' implies also 'your will'. It can be taken in a very narrow way to mean your rules and commandments, seeing them only as tramlines along which we may safely run, without any need for further thought, meditation, decision, application to delicate situations, or even any particular personal and mature involvement.

We have suffered a great deal from this defective conception. The word of God that should bring enlightenment, inspiration, joy, insight into the mysterious working of God in human life and his particular will for each of us can be reduced to mere rules of thumb for a safe passage to heaven. So we may think.

And yet, absolute obedience to the word of God, when we know it, is indispensable. This is part of the 'obedience of faith' St Paul talks about (Rom 1.5), and which he defines as the object of his call to preach. We need to be familiar with the word of God and know where to look for it. The centurion's faith in the word of Christ was rewarded with a miracle and our Lord held him up as an example to all. The Church, indeed, has taken this gentile to her heart and used him as her model at one of her most sacred moments; 'Lord, I am not worthy to receive you, but only say the word, and I shall be healed'.

Peter began his career as an apostle when he obeyed the word of the Lord. Everything argued against it: 'Master, we toiled all night and took nothing! But at your word I will let down the nets' (Lk 5.5). Even the wayward fish came under the spell and direction of the word of Christ. Here we have another image of the Church. Not just Peter, but the whole of nature came under the control and guidance of the creative word of Christ. Peter was to become a fisher of men. Into his net were to come innumerable fish. And the instrument would be the word of God.

The Vatican Council has strongly affirmed the fundamental importance of the word of God for the beginning and the development of faith through which the community of the People of God is first established and then built up.

For through the saving word the spark of faith is struck in unbelievers, and fed in the hearts of the faithful. By this faith, the community of the faithful begins and grows. As the Apostle says: 'Faith depends on hearing, and hearing on the word of Christ' (Rom 10.17) (*The Ministry of Priests*, n. 4).

One of the most characteristic features of the renewal in

theology, preaching and spiritual life in the Church today is the attention given to the word of God. Our principal interest here is in preaching in the ordinary sense in which we use that term; but pulpit-preaching by priests is only one form of the ministry of the word in the Church, as I hope to show. The responsibility for the word of God and for its transmission rests upon all members of the People of God, though this responsibility and its public exercise applies to different people in different ways according to their talent, capacity and office in the Church.

This renewal reflects a need, and the roots of our need lie in our historical situation. A fundamental tenet of the Protestant Reformation was its reliance on the absolute authority of the Bible as the only source of the word of God, and the only liturgical function of the ordained minister was found in the preaching of the word. Although these extreme positions reflected valuable insights that were already present in the late medieval Church, the unhappy consequence was an over-emphasis in Catholic circles in the opposite direction, and from this over-emphasis we have suffered up to the present. Fr Bouyer writes:

There... is no doubt that the development of the Protestant Reformation very soon led only too many Catholics to look on 'Biblicism' in itself as dangerous, as the source, or at any rate the natural environment of heresies. That those religious thinkers who had fallen away from allegiance to the Church had started as the most ardent and effective promoters of the Biblical renewal undoubtedly had the sad result of compromising for a long period the chances in the Catholic Church of a spirituality and theology revivified by fresh recourse to the Bible (*The Word, Church, and Sacraments*, p. 22).

The movement of renewal is now under way, not only in the greater concentration on scripture and its way of thought by the professional theologians, but also at the level of the classroom, the pulpit, and daily devotion and piety. It may not yet have reached all the grass roots, but in many areas of catholic life, the Second Vatican Council has pointed the way. We can compare, for instance, the treatment of such a practical affair as the season of Lent in the encyclical *Mediator Dei* in 1947 with what we find in the *Liturgy Constitution* of Vatican II in 1963. That relatively brief spell of sixteen years shows a quite remarkable change of mood and emphasis. In *Mediator Dei,* we read:

At Septuagesima and during Lent our Mother the Church urges us again and again to meditate on our unhappy condition, to make a powerful effort to amend our lives, to detest our sins above all things and get rid of them by prayer and penance; for it is by continual prayer and repentance for our sins that we obtain God's help, without which all our works are of no avail (C.T.S., n. 168).

Of course, we would not think of questioning the orthodoxy of what is said here, but isn't its accent uninspiring to say the least? It is exclusively moralistic. That is to say, it focusses attention on man's efforts, necessary as they may be, and asks us to reform our way of life. It holds out a rather naked prospect of 'amendment' whilst we meditate upon our 'unhappy condition'. If we do well, God will give us the grace to do good works. It seems fair to say this text gives too much attention to keeping rules of behaviour, and sees the grace of God as offered to those who try hard. That grace will then serve the purpose of keeping them on the right lines. We are perhaps being unfair to the encyclical as a whole, since it contains much rich material on the doctrine of the Mystical Body and the theology of the liturgy, and at the time it marked a great step forward; but it does tend to fall back on a man-centred and rather doleful moralism, where Christian life is seen as keeping rules and commandments.

By contrast, we read in the *Liturgy Constitution* of Vatican II:

The season of Lent has a twofold character; primarily by recalling or preparing for baptism and penance, it disposes the faithful who persevere in hearing the word of God and in prayer, to celebrate the paschal mystery (n. 109).

We are not concerned to go into the many rich insights that are contained here and in the rest of the section on Lent, but only to point out the significant emphasis given to hearing the word of God as an instrument of the yearly renewal of Catholic life. We can, however, note in passing that it does not merely tell us to do our duty and leave it at that; Christian behaviour is placed in the setting of the paschal mystery and baptism, the fundamental realities that with faith constitute our very condition as Christians. These mysteries contain the wellsprings of Christian living.

The texts we have compared are symptomatic of a whole change of mentality in our day. This is important for preaching in any form. For it is from such texts that preachers who voice the word of God in the Church should derive their material. Many neglect them. Their utterance therefore lacks contemporary relevance and inspiration. The Vatican text has a wholly different ring about it. It should influence eventually the whole tone of Catholic life and piety.

We said the *Mediator Dei* text was 'moralizing'. This is a great temptation for preachers. It is too easy. Almost any subject can be made the vehicle for a moralizing sermon. I once heard a sermon on St Athanasius, the great fourth-century theologian at the Council of Nicaea. Within a few sentences, the sermon became a sermon on birth control and communism. The logic is simple. Athanasius tackled the main problems of his day. Our main problems are birth control and communism, and so we are off the mark with our sermon. With this kind of logic the same sermon could be preached every Sunday, and it often is. It could take the form: 'You must go to Mass on Sunday', or 'You must send your children to Catholic schools', or 'You must be sorry for your sins',

11

or 'Go regularly to communion and confession'. I am not saying such things should not be urged from the pulpit, or that sermons should never be moralizing or practical. But if they are restricted regularly in this way to matters of practice, the spiritual diet is lean and the result is an under-nourished faith which will fail to support the practice.

In point of fact, the moral life itself requires sustenance from the word of God, and this, again, is the accent of Vatican II:

The first, and most necessary gift is that charity by which we love God above all things, and our neighbour because of God. If that love, as a good seed, is to grow and bring forth fruit in the soul, each one of the faithful must willingly hear the word of God and with the help of his grace act to fulfil his will (*The Church*, n. 42).

We might notice in passing that this attention given to the word of God shifts the accent and focus from man and what man has to do. His moral life, in the sense of his general behaviour and activity as a Christian, is seen not merely as a set of rules to be followed, though indeed there are rules to be followed, but as a response to the word of God. It is God's direction and light that comes first.

Perhaps in the *Constitution on Divine Revelation* the Council's interest in the theme of the word of God is most strikingly expressed. The document has this to say about the importance of the word of God for Christian life. Here it is referring specifically to the scriptures:

For in the sacred books, the Father who is in heaven meets his children with great love and speaks with them; and the force and power in the word of God is so great that it remains the support and energy of the Church, the strength of faith for her sons, the food of the soul, the pure and perennial source of spiritual life (n. 21).

Some practical effects of this awareness are already evident in the way Mass is now celebrated. The readings in the first part of the Mass are spoken from a lectern or ambo separated from the altar in order that due solemnity and prominence be given to the liturgical action of proclaiming the word of God. The new Lectionary provides a better selection of readings, with more readings from the Old Testament and a more varied cycle spread over several years. It is also well understood that the whole renewal of liturgical worship will depend on the faithful becoming more familiar with the word of God as we find it in the written scriptures:

Sacred Scripture is of paramount importance in the celebration of the liturgy. For it is from Scripture that lessons are read and explained in the homily, and psalms are sung; the prayers, collects and liturgical songs are scriptural in their inspiration, and it is from scripture that actions and signs derive their meaning. Thus, if the restoration, progress and adaptation of the sacred liturgy are to be achieved, it is necessary to promote that warm and living love for Scripture to which the venerable tradition of both Eastern and Western rites give testimony (*Liturgy Constitution*, n. 24).

Briefly, then, I have indicated how the word of God is basic to Christian life, and how today in the Church there is a growing awareness of that fact. Through the word of God, through 'hearing', we come to first faith and to growth in faith; it is the word that assembles the People of God and nourishes them once assembled; the life of charity, Christian behaviour, is fed and sustained through meditation on the word of God; God speaks to us and deals with us familiarly in the pages of scripture; our worship is basically a response to the word of God, and is enriched by our familiarity with his word in scripture, for

in the liturgy God speaks to his people, and Christ is still proclaiming his gospel. And the people reply to God both by song and prayer (*ibid*. n. 33).

All this happens in the Church and through the Church. Herself created and fashioned by the word, she remains its true minister, for her own children and for those outside. Like Mary, she carries in her womb the word of life which she brings forth in every generation. All her members have their part to play in transmitting the word of God for the salvation of all.

I have used the term 'word of God' in many different senses, and these I hope to clarify in due course. But first we must ask: why is the word of God so important? To answer this, we look first to the sources of faith in the scriptures.

CHAPTER II

THE LIVING WORD

But first we have a practical difficulty. In the world we live in words have become a debased coinage. The mass media, television, radio, advertisement, the over-abundance of print, all contribute to making us less word-conscious than our forebears. We have become less sensitive to what is said. This all affects the preaching of the gospel. We are too used to being 'got at'. Everybody wants to gain our attention and persuade us of something, whether it be a political programme or the advantages of a particular brand of soap. The result is that we find it increasingly difficult to listen to anything for any length of time. We are conditioned to shorter and sharper stimuli. The long sermon, for instance, is a thing of the past. Altogether we take words far less seriously. There are too many of them around.

The word, in fact, has tended to become divorced from the person who speaks. We read newspapers, but are not particularly concerned to know our editor. We pick up a book in the library, but the author is only a name to us. The words, we feel, are not addressed to us as persons, as people. They are more addressed to our minds. They give information or provide distraction. They do not necessarily involve us with the author in a personal way.

Some would trace the roots of our attitude to the influence of Greek civilization in western culture – thus making a sharp contrast with the way of thought of the semitic peoples who wrote the Bible. With the Greeks words are the fruit of the human intelligence extracting from things their essential nature and qualities, and their relationships with other things. They then become the vehicle of communication between minds. They pass on this knowledge of things. F. X. Arnold writes:

The Greek Logos (word) is the expression of thought, of the idea of a *thing*. It hardly applies to the person. It is not a way of speaking to him, a word that acts upon a man; it is rather the expression of a thing. The Greek Logos is word, discourse, manifestation, revelation, not in the sense that it announces something one should give serious attention to in a personal way, but in the sense that it describes something one should recognize and understand (F. X. Arnold, *Proclamation de la Foi et Communauté de Foi*, p. 23. Here he summarizes Kleinknecht in the Dictionary of Kittel).

On the other hand, the word in the Bible is not primarily concerned with 'things' but with people. It is more concerned with their will than their mind, with their moral response, than their information, though the opening up of the mind is necessarily included. The word in the Bible demands submission and acceptance. And it is imbued with creative power.

It is the manifestation of a will, an active power, a creative activity of God towards man and towards his people. The 'dabar Jahweh', the hebrew 'word', of the Old Testament, like the 'Logos tou Theou', the word of God, of the New Testament is a powerful force which is decisive in history and in the history of salvation (*ibid.* p. 24).

So we find it is the word of God that creates: 'And God

15

said: "Let there be light"; and there was light' (Gen 1.3).

O God of my Fathers and Lord of Mercy,
who hast made all things by thy word,
and by thy wisdom hast formed man (Wis 9.1).

By the word of the Lord the heavens were made,
And all their hosts by the breath of his mouth...
For he spoke, and it came to be;
He commanded and it stood forth (Ps 33.6,9).

The word of God gives life where it is received, and in
doing so accomplishes the designs of God:

For as the rain and the snow come down from heaven
and return not thither but water the earth,
making it bud forth and sprout,
giving seed to the sower and bread to the eater,
so shall my word be that goes forth from my mouth;
it shall not return to me empty,
but it shall accomplish that which I purpose,
and prosper in the thing for which I sent it (Is 55.10,11).

The word of God can bring healing:

Some were sick through their sinful ways
and because of their iniquities suffered affliction...
Then they cried to the Lord in their trouble
and he delivered them from their distress;
he sent forth his word, and healed them,
and delivered them from destruction (Ps 107.17,19,20).

Sometimes it appears as personified and acting for God.
Besides healing and saving, it can also bring destruction
and condemnation:

For while a gentle silence enveloped all things,
And night in its swift course was now half-gone,
thy all-powerful word leaped from heaven, from the royal throne,
into the midst of a land that was doomed,
a stern warrior carrying the sharp sword of thy authentic

command,
and stood and filled all things with death,
and touched heaven while standing on the earth (Wis 18.14-16).

We find the same in the New Testament, though the significance is deepened and enriched through the coming of Jesus Christ. The word of God, now the gospel, is seen as a dynamic reality again acting for God and achieving his purposes. It is fruitful, creative, powerful, bringing wisdom, challenging and distinguishing those who receive and those who reject.

It gives life: 'you have the words of eternal life' (Jn 6.68); it saves: 'receive with meekness the implanted word which is able to save your souls' (Jas 1.21); gives rebirth: 'you have been born anew, not of perishable seed but of imperishable, through the living and abiding word of God' (1 Pet 1.23); it makes us free: 'if you continue in my word, you are truly my disciples, and you will know the truth, and the truth will make you free' (Jn 8.31); it grows and becomes strong (Acts 19.20), and is multiplied (Acts 12.24); it is an active force: 'when you received the word of God which you heard from us, you accepted it not as the word of men but as what it really is, the word of God, which is at work in you believers' (1 Thess 2.13); it runs and is victorious: 'pray for us, that the word of the Lord may speed on and triumph as it did among you' (2 Thess 3.1); it has a life of its own independent of the preacher: 'the gospel for which I am suffering and wearing fetters like a criminal. But the word of God is not fettered' (2 Tim 2.9); it reconciles God and man (2 Cor 5.19); it is like a sword in the hand of God: 'for the word of God is living and active, sharper than any two-edged sword, piercing to the division of the soul and spirit, of joints and marrow, and discerning the thoughts and intentions of the heart' (Heb 4.12).

The virtue and force here attributed to the word of God is only intelligible if God himself is personally active when his word is heard. It implies not only the external act of proclamation of the word, but also the internal activity of the Holy Spirit disposing the hearer to accept the word presented to him externally. Thus the word becomes the medium of personal communion.

The manifold phrases and images employed in the scripture to describe the efficacy of the word are various attempts by way of word-pictures to help us see something of what happens in the order of grace when we enter into a personal communion with God. The terms are apt, for this is the function of language. People have to communicate by words or signs. This is how they reveal to other people what is in their minds and hearts and intention. With man we can be deceived. There need not necessarily be a commitment of the person. But with God no deception is possible. His word, once delivered, 'abides for ever' (Is 40.8), and the psalmist can pray:

I wait for the Lord, my soul waits,
and in his word I hope;
For with the Lord there is steadfast love (Ps 130.5,7).

And so, when God speaks, it is not merely an idea of himself he communicates, or a series of statements about himself that can become the object of a detached intellectual consideration. This is not the knowledge of God that he offers through his word of revelation. It is not just a word about God, but God himself speaking and addressing the person and inviting him to the kind of knowledge that implies the acceptance of a personal relationship. We call this acceptance faith, hope, and charity. The *Decree on Revelation* of Vatican II says of the word of God in scripture: 'in the sacred books, the Father who is in heaven meets his children with great love and speaks with them' (*Revelation*, n. 21). And in the liturgy Constitution we read that when the sacred scriptures are read in Church, Christ himself 'is present in his word, since it is he himself who speaks when the holy Scriptures are read in the church' (*Liturgy*, n. 7).

Karl Rahner writes of the modern approaches to the treatise on grace:

The present-day discussion on grace is leaving aside a too material concept of grace to stress its personal element – primarily
understood as the uncreated selfcommunication of God – and is
thus finding an approach to the word of God and a more com-
prehensive understanding of it, regarding it as the means whereby a person discloses himself and freely imparts himself to another (*Theological Investigations*, volume IV, p. 256).

The decisive word of God to the people of Israel is described as a covenant. This means a kind of pact or
agreement between people. It committed both sides, if
we can use that term of God. On God's part there was a
promise to which he would be eternally faithful. On the
part of the people there was a promise to be faithful to
his word, particularly as expressed in the law. In this way
the word of God entered history and became a living force
that shaped and fashioned the people of Israel. This
word was treasured in their community and lovingly
meditated upon; it became the law of life; it gave direction and meaning to their history.

We find several covenants with the patriarchs. After
the first promise of salvation in Genesis 3.15, sometimes
referred to as the first announcing of the gospel, we have
the covenants with Noah (Gen 9.8ff.), Abraham (Gen
17.1), Isaac (Gen 26.2-4), Jacob (Gen 28.13). But the
decisive event for the people of Israel was their libera-
tion from Egypt and the relationship established through
Moses and through the word of God that came to him
on Mount Sinai:

And Moses went up to God, and the Lord called to him out of
the mountain, saying, 'Thus you shall say to the house of Jacob,
and tell the people of Israel: you have seen what I did to the
Egyptians, and how I bore you on eagles' wings and brought
you to myself. Now therefore, if you will obey my voice and
keep my covenant, you shall be my own possession among all
peoples; for all the earth is mine, and you shall be to me a kingdom of priests and a holy nation. These are the words you shall
speak to the children of Israel' (Exod 19.3-6).

Running through the whole of the Old Testament is the tradition that the covenant is the expression of a special love of God for his chosen people. Later writings, especially Hosea, use the symbol of married love to express this relationship. Similarly in Deuteronomy we find:

It was not because you were more in number than any other people that the Lord set his love upon you and chose you, for you were the fewest of all peoples; but it was because the Lord loves you, and is keeping the oath which he swore to your fathers (Deut 7.7,8).

The communication of the word of God was thus for the People of God a decisive event. It had far-reaching consequences. It was not merely sound or intellectual conception detached from the person who uttered the word, as is the case with so many human words. It was God expressing his will in a way that involved a promise and a design. And it established the relationship of love. Through the word of God breaking into their history, Israel became the People of God.

CHAPTER III

GOD SPEAKS THROUGH MEN

The people came to a knowledge and love of God through the preaching of the prophets, Moses in particular. The word 'prophet' does not primarily mean one who foretells the future, though in fact that was a part of their function, but one who is an accredited spokesman, who 'speaks out'. The people only heard the voice of God from afar. The prophets delivered the message. They were equipped for their mission by the gift of a special insight and calling, a special gift of the spirit of God. This gift was given for the people, and in fulfilling their task of communication the prophets fulfilled their own special destiny. Their word became the word of God.

Herein lies a basic mystery of God's dealng with man. It is easy to say the word of the prophet was the word of God, just as it is easy to say the preacher preaches the word of God, but the fact is this leaves the word of God open to the vagaries of human weakness and imperfection. The inspiration of scripture is a special case, of course, where God himself assures the authenticity of what is said, but even there a human element appears which presents difficulties. For the moment, I am only concerned to make the point that God has chosen to speak through the medium of human words and actions. It is a part of what is called 'the economy of salvation'. God could have acted in other ways. He chose this.

God spoke sometimes through individuals, and sometimes through the life of the community where his word was preserved. Their liturgy, their law, their accumulated wisdom, served to preserve the word of God for future generations and to shape the life of the community. The word thus became part of the 'institution'. But that God did speak through the words of men is the basic point, and this is the evidence of scripture.

That the prophet speaks the words of God is conveyed in many striking picture-stories. There is a great reverence for the voice of God himself. The people say they will die if they hear the voice of God, and ask Moses to go into God's presence for them: 'You speak to us and we will hear; but let not God speak to us lest we die' (Exod 20.19). Moses has already declared himself unwilling since he is no good as a speaker, but he is told that he will be given the necessary help:

'Oh, my Lord, I am not eloquent, either heretofore or since thou hast spoken to thy servant; but I am slow of speech and of tongue'. Then the Lord said to him: 'Who has made man's mouth? Who makes him dumb, or deaf, or seeing or blind? Is it not I, the Lord? Now therefore go, and I will be with your mouth and teach you what you shall speak' (Exod 4.10-12).

So, God is able to communicate his word even through weak instruments.

The position of Moses among the prophets is unique. He is a prophet in a class of his own.

A passage in the Book of Numbers shows Aaron and his wife claiming equality with Moses because they too are prophets and have received the word of God. God says to them:

Hear my words: if there is a prophet among you, I the Lord make myself known to him in a vision, I speak with him in a dream. Not so with my servant Moses; he is entrusted with all my house. With him I speak mouth to mouth and not in dark speech; and he beholds the form of the Lord (Num 12.6).

We can notice that there can be several grades of capacity to preach the word of God. Moses was more than an ordinary prophet. His function in the history of God's dealing with the people was original and, as it were, archetypal. There is here a foreshadowing of the New Testament and the new covenant where the decisive word is spoken in Jesus Christ, who alone has 'seen the Father'. Similarly, in their degree, the apostles had a unique function and were specially equipped because they had known the Lord and conversed with him and were witnesses to all he had said and accomplished.

The prophets commonly feel themselves inadequate to the task of speaking in the name of God. Isaiah considers his lips to be sullied and they are purified with a burning coal in his vision of the divine majesty (Is 6.5ff.). This vision is still referred to in the Mass in the prayer *Munda Cor* which the priest recites before reading the holy words of the gospel. Jeremiah claims he is a child who cannot speak, but 'the Lord put forth his hand and touched my mouth', with the consequence:

Behold, I have put my words in your mouth.
See, I have set you this day over the nations and over kingdoms,
to pluck up and to break down,
to destroy and overthrow,
to build and to plant (Jer 1.9,10).

Jeremiah's speech is invested with the power of the word of God.

Sometimes they are compelled almost against their will to prophesy (Jonah; Ezek 33.22; Jer 20.9; 6.11; Amos 3.8). They are aware that their speech is God's own word which they are charged to deliver. In his vision, Ezekiel is given a scroll with words written upon it which he is bidden to eat: ' "Son of man, eat this scroll which I give you and fill your stomach with it." Then I ate it; and it was in my mouth as sweet as honey' (Ezek 3.3). In these striking ways the point is made that when the prophet speaks he speaks in the name of God with the words of God.

On the other hand, although the prophets are conscious of being used by God, yet their writings show that they exercise their own literary and creative talents. They bear the stamp of individual personalities and temperaments. The prophet is not an irrational tool, an ecstatic unaware of what he is saying. There is an interplay between the inspiration of God and the free co-operation of man. It is necessary to bear this in mind in any theology of preaching today, for the efficacy of the word can be limited by the imperfect co-operation of the preacher.

When the prophet, whether he be under the old law or the new, ceases to subordinate himself to God, then his utterance ceases to be the word of God and becomes simply the word of man. In particular, the false prophets are unable to recognize evil, even though they may be sincere, and they simply pander to the people's preferences instead of denouncing abuses:

I did not send the prophets,
yet they ran;
I did not speak to them,
yet they prophesied.
I have heard what the prophets have said who prophesy in my name, saying: 'I have dreamed, I have dreamed'. Let the prophet who has a dream tell the dream, but let him who has my word speak my word faithfully. Behold I am against the prophets, says the Lord, who use their tongues and say, 'Says the Lord'. Behold I am against those who prophesy lying dreams, says the Lord... (Jer 23.21,25,28,31,32).

At the beginning of his career, the prophet receives his commission from God. It is usually presented in some dramatic way. He is called and sent. This implies a special experience of the word of God, a gift which, especially in the later prophets is attributed to the spirit of God coming upon the prophet. In the Old Testament we cannot yet attribute the personal identity of the Holy Spirit to this more general use of the term 'spirit', but even there a time is foretold by the prophets themselves when the spirit of God will be poured out in abundance: 'and on my menservants and my maidservants in those days I will pour out my Spirit; and they shall prophesy' (Joel 2.30). St Peter calls attention to this prophecy in Acts 2 on the day of Pentecost, seeing it there fulfilled in the Church; and indeed St Luke is particularly interested in showing the Holy Spirit at work in the Church directing her preaching and inspiring the new prophets, the preachers of the gospel.

At this point we can draw some conclusions for the modern preacher or prophet, whether he be priest or layman. Given the freedom of man, it is possible for a prophet to be false. The first duty of the preacher, therefore is to be faithful to the objective word of God as it has been revealed, and as it may be found in the traditions of the People of God. Secondly, he must be faithful to the gift of the Spirit he receives as a Christian or as an ordained minister, the Spirit who is promised to assist him in the preaching of the gospel in the community of the People of God. If he is faithful in this way, his preaching can then be said to be a participation in the love God bestows on his people.

However, how are the people to tell that the prophet is not merely speaking his own words, the word of man, but the very word of God?

In the Old Testament and in the New, the voice of the prophet or preacher is often authenticated by a miracle, or extraordinary event. This may act as a sign that God, the author of miracles, supports his utterance. Those who have faith can recognize the event, the sign, for what it means, and see into its significance, and their reaction is one of wonder and astonishment and reverence at this presence of God. The event lends authority to the speaker. The draught of fish brings Peter to his knees and makes him listen to our Lord's invitation to follow him. Our Lord cures the paralytic as a sign that he has the power also to heal spiritual paralysis. He raises Lazarus, and explains: 'I am the resurrection and the life' (Jn 11.25). Similar extraordinary events attend and confirm the preaching of the apostles in the book of Acts.

The prophet or preacher is not on his own. He is a part of a tradition, and that tradition is not made up only of words in the ordinary sense of speech or writing. In fact the principal way in which God has manifested his will and providence is through his great deeds, the wonderful works, events, actions, on behalf of the people. The function of the prophet and preacher is principally to point to these great deeds and explain their significance to the faith of the people. So the Vatican Council states that the principal characteristic of preaching at Mass should be that of:

a proclamation of God's wonderful works in the history of salvation, that is, the mystery of Christ, which is ever made present and active within us, especially in the celebration of the liturgy (*Liturgy*, n. 35.2).

This directive in its turn is based on the characteristics of the manner of God's self-revelation and his plan for mankind the way he has 'spoken' through events and the word of his accredited prophets in revelation as a whole. The decree on revelation sums it up as follows:

This plan of revelation is realized by deeds and words having an inner unity; the deeds wrought by God in the history of salvation manifest the teaching and the realities signified by the words, while the words proclaim the deeds and clarify the mystery contained in them (*Revelation*, n. 2).

We must, of course, distinguish that function of prophecy where the words of the prophet actually form a part of revelation itself in its constitutive or foundational stage. The inspired words of the Old Testament writers belong to the 'deposit of faith', as do the writings of the New Testament. But even the modern people of God whose task it is to pass on the tradition and announce it to the modern world will still be committed basically to 'proclaiming the wonderful works of God in the history of salvation' as a norm of authenticity, and the modern preacher must be able to find in his own utterance this content of the word of God, though indeed it has to be applied to particular congregations and to particular historical situations. Further, the witness of his own and the people's way of life, his moral rectitude, his endurance under persecution,—all these supported the words of the prophets and the same laws apply today. Finally, as we now know, it is the work of the Holy Spirit to give an affinity of soul, his interior witness, his gift of wisdom, whereby the hearers are able, in the light of external testimony, to recognize and accept the word of God coming from the mouth of the preacher.

CHAPTER IV

GOD'S FIRST AND LAST WORD

The word of God that was announced through the prophets, the wonderful works of God in the Old Testament —all find their completion and fulfilment in Jesus Christ. In him are 'all the treasures of assured understanding and the knowledge of God's mystery, of Christ, in whom are hid all the treasures of wisdom and knowledge' (Col 2.2,3). We can expect no new public revelation. The last days are here that will last to the end of the world. For,

Jesus perfected revelation by fulfilling it through his whole work of making himself and manifesting himself; through his words and deeds, his signs and wonders, but especially through his death and glorious resurrection from the dead and final sending of the Spirit of truth (*Revelation*, n. 4).

The fact that these are the 'last days' sets the stage and provides the context for the preaching of the Church today. The Lord has 'come', the kingdom is established, the victory is won, in a radical and definitive sense. Christian preaching must necessarily look back to the appearance and manifestation of God in Christ, look forward in hope and joy to his reappearance and final manifestation at the end of time, and at the same time bring to its hearers an awareness of the nearness and the presence of Christ in his Church today. It is the task of the Church, through her many preachers, to announce and proclaim this salvation in the present and to give hope for the future. The Lord has said, 'Behold, I am with you', and he has also said, 'Behold, I come'. The contemporary history of the People of God is a history of the Lord's coming, progressively realized in their daily living. A necessary function of Christian preaching is to lead into the consciousness of the abiding presence and power of Christ in the Church. It will announce and proclaim this mystery, and the very announcing, through the power of the Spirit, will contribute to its deeper accomplishment.

Thus the event of preaching is itself a 'sign of the times'. The fact that it is done at all, and that it is accepted in faith, announces the new state of affairs, the new creation, the direction of the life of the Christian community. The person of Jesus Christ remains the centre of its message, the ground of its hope, the source of its strength. When preaching loses that focus and that context, it degenerates into mere words of men. It does not mediate the living and creative word of revelation. It becomes spurious and irrelevant.

Let the prophet who has a dream tell the dream, but let him who has my word speak my word faithfully (Jer 23.25).

In many and various ways God spoke of old to our fathers by the prophets; but in these last days he has spoken to us by a son, whom he appointed heir of all things, through whom also he created the world (Heb 1.1,2).

So the author of Hebrews speaks of God's first and last word, the alpha and omega of all God's words. He is the original word of God, pre-existing from all eternity in the bosom of the Father. The word was 'with God' from the beginning, and is now 'made flesh' and dwells amongst us (Jn 1.14). He 'reflects the glory of God and bears the very stamp of his nature' (Heb 1.3). He eternally reflects and images the Father. Therefore, the words he speaks as man are not his own, but have their origin in the Father, such is the union between them:

For I have not spoken on my own authority; the Father who sent me has himself given commandment what to say and what to speak. And I know that his commandment is eternal life. What I say, therefore, I say as the Father has bidden me (Jn 12.49,50).

Christ's word not only reveals, but also gives life and access to the Father: 'nobody can come to the Father except through me' (Jn 14.6). In his very person and in his actions he reveals the Father: 'He who has seen me has seen the Father; how can you say, "Show us the Father"? Do you not believe that I am in the Father and the Father in me?... The Father who dwells in me does his works' (Jn 14. 9-10).

Here are the roots of Christian preaching. The word of the preacher derives its power from its ultimate source in the Word that is eternally uttered and has now been made manifest. Preaching shares in that manifestation. It is therefore in very reality a form of participation in the activity of the Blessed Trinity. The Word eternally goes forth, yet never leaves the Father's side, and returns heavy-laden. It does not 'return to me empty' (Is 55.11), but is at work through the power of the Holy Spirit to reform and reshape man in the image of his Creator. Not only must the content of Christian preaching, therefore, insofar as it is subject to conceptual analysis and systematic arrangement, be clearly rooted in the Trinity, but also the preacher himself, and the people who listen, need the consciousness in faith of this basic mystery, the foundation of all belief and Christian existence.

Whenever we speak of the Word of God, we are involved with this mystery. The Word made flesh has opened up for us the interior life of God. Through faith in the Word, we enter the kingdom of love, and rejoice in its hope and in its power. Christ, 'the Word made flesh', is 'the way, the truth, and the life' (Jn 14.6).

Many preachers and teachers are afraid to preach about the Blessed Trinity. It is as though this were a special section of doctrine only to be handled by experts, a special chapter on its own not always dealt with when you don't get through the syllabus. This is the danger when preaching or teaching simply takes a system of doctrinal statements for its basis. One section can get isolated from the rest. Bits can get left out. Other bits can receive undue emphasis and length of treatment. An organic view of the whole with proper proportion of parts can be spoiled, as in one of those funny mirrors. And yet the Trinity is the basis of everything. It can never be left out.

But we do have a difficulty. For centuries theologians have tried to unravel something of this mystery as it is revealed to us. These writings can become exceedingly complex and hard to follow. Today, many people, religious educators, professors of theology, preachers, are seeking to clarify the relationship between this kind of refined intellectual analysis, which is in itself very necessary, and the day-to-day faith of the Christian. For teaching and preaching purposes it is not enough to extract 'doctrine', a series of statements about God in an abstract form from the sources of revelation, and then hand on this content of structured ideas. At least not enough by itself, as, for example, in the days when the old-style catechism was the staple diet in the classroom. There must be a return to the Word of God himself, where he speaks to us and meets us and invites us to love and communion of life. The teacher or preacher must see his function as a mediator, to a certain extent discreetly on the side-lines, who by his words and technique helps to place the hearer before God himself. For

God is ever present in his word, which, in the Church, can take many forms. At the same time, sound theological doctrine makes the original word more explicit, adapts its structures and forms of expression to the needs of contemporary man, and communicates the mature and developed meditation of the Church on the word committed to her care. It also provides sure lines of interpretation and is a very necessary activity, but it has tended in recent years to become too much the province of the specialist theologian and to become too far removed from the living faith of the people.

One way in which this discussion is resolved is to say that all Christian proclamation should be 'kerygmatic', that is to say, it should contain a message for faith, a direct appeal to religious commitment. To say this is not to do away with the proper function of the scientific theologian, but even he should have an eye on the practical implications of what he says. In the gospels the word used for preaching is the Greek word *kerussein* which means to announce or to act as herald. From this comes the noun *kerygma* which means the content of what is announced. In the gospels this preaching is manifestly aimed at the religious commitment in faith of the hearers. They accept or reject. They are placed before a decision. Similarly, it is argued, in matters of Christian belief there is not much point in teaching a logically co-ordinated system of theological ideas, which any pagan could learn, if it does not apply to life, if it does not make an appeal to the person as such. Somehow this theology must 'come alive', mediate a message to the hearers, and lead to personal communion with the Trinity. It must also maintain the keynote of hope and joy which is the characteristic of the Good News of the gospel. Both among teachers of religion in schools and students of the pastoral preaching of priests, it is felt that teaching and preaching will benefit best from giving closer attention to the theology of the word of God in its

31

many implications.

Fr Ratzinger has this to say about preaching on the Trinity:

Our preaching would not be trinitarian if, in expounding the Trinity, it did so speculatively, yet excluded the Christian's existence in that Trinity... Ontological statements of dogma [i.e. about reality in the abstract], though absolutely necessary for the orthodoxy of the faith, remain peripheral safeguards when it comes to preaching. They are not central themes (Joseph Ratzinger, 'Christocentric Preaching' in Symposium *The Word*, p. 209).

The central theme is the history of salvation and the centre of that history is the mystery of Christ. When we say 'mystery', we do not mean simply something we do not understand. St Paul uses the word of Christ in the sense that there has been in history a hidden reality, a presence at work which is the hand of God. The words and works of God in the history of the people of Israel said something about Christ, prepared the way for his coming, were a part of his 'mystery'. Similarly today the mystery of Christ is present and active in the Church. The Church is Christ present and active in his members through the gift of the Holy Spirit. He is its hidden reality. It is these events and actions of God in history, together with the words that explain them, that are the groundwork and basic content of Christian preaching. First God spoke in the Old Testament, showing himself as one God. Then Christ appeared declaring himself to be the son and promising to send the Holy Spirit in his name. These are the facts together with the Lord's life, death and resurrection and the sending of the Spirit. Doctrine works upon these facts to elucidate and clarify the problems of understanding. But the basis of proclamation, as of faith, is the history itself as it is significant and effective for our salvation.

In the scene at the baptism in the Jordan, our Lord is shown to have a special relationship with the Father and the Holy Spirit. He is also the prophet of whom Moses spoke: 'I will raise up for them a prophet like you from among their brethren; and I will put words in his mouth and he shall speak to them all that I shall command him' (Deut 18.18). The heavens open, the voice of God is heard to claim him as his Son and the Spirit is seen to descend upon him 'like resting upon like' (Cyril of Jerusalem, *On the Mysteries,* III.1). Our Lord is already introduced by the preaching of John the Baptist, a significant figure appearing like a typical Old Testament prophet, and so pointing to the continuity of our Lord's task with the word of God in the Old Testament.

A similar scene occurs at the moment of the transfiguration. A significant detail is added. Here our Lord is seen conversing with Moses and Elijah, who represent the era of the law and the prophets. At the same time the glory with which he is surrounded and the presence of the 'cloud' that indicates the Spirit of God show him to be unique: 'and a cloud overshadowed them, and a voice came out of the cloud, "This is my beloved Son; listen to him" ' (Mk 9.7).

Christ, the Word of God to man, can be seen, then, from two points of view: as the eternal Word coming forth from the bosom of the Father, or as the final word that sums up all the other words of God in the history of salvation. In either case the person of Christ is at the centre. Christian preaching must 'listen to him' primarily and always. It is not only Trinitarian, but also centred on Christ. This would seem to be obvious, but preachers and teachers are not always aware of its implications. It is part of the thinking that has determined the renewal of devotion along the lines of the Bible and the liturgy in the Church, for Christ and his mystery, 'ever made present and active within us, especially in the celebration of the liturgy' (*Liturgy*, n. 35), is at the heart of the Bible and the Church's worship. Catholic devotion and piety have drawn too often and too much on secondary sources, good in themselves, but, if overstressed, injurious to the principle of christocentrism. They can therefore become substitutes which only imperfectly feed Christian faith and life. Even devotion to the saints or to our Lady can get out of focus. Doctrinal teaching too can lack organic unity. Grace, for instance, can be presented as a thing which makes us holy, but is detached from participation in the mystery of Christ. The sacraments can 'give grace', but not be thought of as actions of Christ. The Church can be simply an institution with an organizational structure, and not thought of as the Body of Christ. Christian death can be seen exclusively as the way to our judgement, to be prepared for accordingly, and not as a participation in the mystery of Christ's Passover from death to life. Keeping the commandments can be detached altogether from a sense of sharing in the mystery of Christ.

When we say preaching is to be centred on Christ in the history of salvation, this includes not only the mystery as achieved in his resurrection and glorification, his paschal mystery, but also Christ as present now in the Church – in other words, the 'whole Christ'. This should give preaching its quality of actuality, and also its proper reference to the community implications of our faith. The whole Christ is the Church. Properly orientated preaching has a major task before it today to correct the excessive individualism that has reigned for so long in Catholic piety. This individualism is beginning to disappear as a result of the greater theological awareness of the Church and of Christ's presence in the Church. The awareness of Christ's presence and action in the Church, his Mystical Body, is also one of the mainsprings of the modern liturgical movement and provides the theological basis for such practical affairs as communal and external participation by way of responses, prayers, and singing:

Liturgical services are not private functions, but are celebrations of the Church, which is 'the sacrament of unity', namely, a holy people united and organized under their bishops.

Therefore liturgical services pertain to the whole body of the Church; they manifest it and have effects upon it... (*Liturgy*, n. 26).

The same reason underlies the directive in the *Constitution* that popular devotions are to maintain a proper relationship with liturgical worship. They should not move too far away from their source in the mystery of Christ which is especially realized in the Church's solemn prayer. Devotions play an important part in the life of the Christian people. Necessarily so. They adapt prayer to the needs of a particular age, and emphasize certain aspects of faith that may be under attack, or be useful for the needs of a given age. Devotion to our Lord under the sign of the love of the Sacred Heart emphasized what was lacking in the Jansenist presentation of God as a severe judge. Devotion to the permanent presence of our Lord in the Blessed Sacrament increased when the doctrine was under attack. But devotions, whilst they emphasize one particular aspect of faith, should act as a window on the whole. They meet the needs and respond to the special feeling of the people, but they should not become substitutes for the faith itself. In particular they should be easily related to the public worship of the Church which expresses that faith. These devotions should be integrated in the mind of the people with the main events and mysteries of the history of salvation, particularly the paschal mystery.

Popular devotions of the Christian people are warmly recommended, provided they accord with the laws and norms of the Church... These devotions should be so drawn up that they harmonize with the liturgical seasons, accord with the sacred liturgy, are in some fashion derived from it, and lead the people to it, since the liturgy by its very nature far surpasses any of them (*Liturgy*, n. 13).

Whilst wishing to encourage popular devotions, the Church is concerned that there should be no imbalance in piety and prayer, for where there is imbalance in prayer, there will also be imbalance in faith. What is of lesser importance receives too much stress and this is injurious to Christian maturity. Public prayer expresses the faith of the Church and therefore it has to be jealously guarded from abuse and excess. The reforming proposals of the Council reflect the imbalances in present-day Catholicism. It is not unknown for people to have houses bedecked with rosaries and crucifixes, and yet to miss Sunday Mass. People will attend the Stations of the Cross on Good Friday, yet will not be present at the solemn reading of the gospel of the Passion and the distribution of Communion and the solemn prayers for the needs of the Church that are part of the liturgical service. They will go to midnight Mass at Christmas–good thing–but hardly be aware of the night service on Holy Saturday where baptismal promises are renewed and the Lord's resurrection is solemnly celebrated. I once took part in a group discussion where I was proposing that there should be more reading of the Bible in Catholic homes. This particular group decided it was impracticable because it would interfere with the family rosary. Some adjustment of values seems necessary.

The Council strongly urges that we get our priorities right in matters of piety and devotion. The directive principle is that Christ in his mysteries should have the central place; particularly the celebration and memorial of his death and resurrection:

By an apostolic tradition which took its origin from the very day of Christ's resurrection, the Church celebrates the paschal mystery every eighth day; with good reason this, then, bears the name of the Lord's day or the day of the Lord... Hence the Lord's day is the original feast-day, and it should be proposed to the piety of the faithful and taught to them in such a way that it may become in fact a day of joy and freedom from work. Other celebrations, unless they be of overriding importance, must not have precedence over this day, which is the foundation and nucleus of the whole liturgical year (*Liturgy*, n. 106).

The importance of the Sunday lies in its commemoration of the great event of the Lord's resurrection. This was the great good news of the apostolic preaching. When we speak of Christ as the centre of the history of salvation, we also mean the great triumph of his life on earth, which was consummated in his resurrection and ascension and glorification in heaven. This is how our salvation was achieved. Without it, our faith is vain. Our participation in the mystery of Christ is a participation in the fruits of his resurrection, particularly the gift of the Spirit. This is summed up in the use of the phrase 'Paschal Mystery', to describe Christ's passing over from death to life, a mystery in which we participate by baptism, and which was foretold in the passing over from bondage to freedom of the People of Israel. In other words, the basic content of Christian preaching can be summed up as our participation in Christ's Paschal Mystery.

A glance at the Council documents will show how central this theme is to the Church's thinking about her redemption. We have already seen the change from *Mediator Dei's* treatment of Lent, which is to be considered now as a preparation for 'celebrating the paschal mystery'. The feasts of the Church are to be revised: 'so that they duly nourish the piety of the faithful who celebrate the mysteries of Christian redemption, and above all the paschal mystery' (*Liturgy*, n. 107). In celebrating the feasts of the saints, 'the Church proclaims the paschal mystery as achieved in the saints who have suffered and who have been glorified with Christ' (*Liturgy*, n. 104).

The wonders wrought by God among the people of the Old Testament were but a prelude to the work of Christ the Lord in redeeming mankind and giving perfect glory to God. He achieved this task principally by the paschal mystery of his blessed passion, resurrection from the dead, and glorious ascension, whereby 'dying he destroyed our death and, rising, he restored our life. For it was from the side of Christ as he slept the sleep of death upon the cross that there came forth the wondrous sacrament with is the whole Church (*Liturgy*, n. 5).

In this way the Council sums up the history of salvation and the paschal mystery. It is to be kept to the forefront of the piety of the faithful and should be the essential content of preaching in whatever form. The Church herself preaches and expresses her faith in her liturgy, and the Council is very careful that that celebration should be centred on the mystery of Christ. For that reason, balance is to be preserved:

The minds of the faithful must be directed primarily towards the feasts of our Lord... Therefore the Proper of the Time shall be given the preference which is due over the feasts of the saints, so that the entire cycle of the mysteries of salvation can be suitably recalled (*ibid*. n. 108).

CHAPTER V

THE WORD MADE PRESENT
THROUGH THE SPIRIT

On the day of Pentecost, the Church that was 'born from the side of Christ as he slept the sleep of death on the cross', (*Liturgy*, n. 5), became 'manifest', and on that day, 'those who received the word [of Peter] were baptized' (Acts 2.41). Aided by the signs of the Spirit's activity all around, Peter pointed to a wonderful work of God. With the assistance, exterior and interior, of the Spirit, the event was accepted as a visitation of God. At the same time Peter's words were substantiated by what was happening before their very eyes. And so his preaching made the mystery known and accepted. Thus was gathered the first community.

Peter's taking on of the role of preacher was itself a significant event. A new era was inaugurated. The outpouring of the Spirit signified a decisive phase of salvation history, when men, both as a community and as individuals, would speak in the name of Christ and make him present. They would share his prophetic mission. They would be anointed by the Spirit, just as he himself was anointed, and by the abiding gift of the Spirit in the Church would prophesy. This anointing comes through Baptism, Confirmation, and Orders. I am using the term 'prophetic' in this general sense here, in the sense that the gift is attached by God to these institutions. Another more special sense of the gift of prophecy refers to a special gift given to individuals for the needs of the Church at a special time.

St Luke and St John give most attention to the mystery of the communication of the 'Spirit of Christ'. Our Lord's own preaching is presented by Luke as prompted by the Spirit, just as the prophets of the Old Testament had been anointed and inspired by the spirit of God. In the synagogue at Nazareth he applies to himself the word of the prophet Isaiah:

The Spirit of the Lord is upon me, because he has anointed me to preach the good news to the poor... And he closed the book, and gave it back to the attendant and sat down; and the eyes of all in the synagogue were fixed on him. And he began to say to them, 'Today this scripture has been fulfilled in your hearing' (Lk 4.18-21).

The scene is written with a certain sense of drama. 'Today this scripture has been fulfilled.' Today. When Christ speaks, something happens. The gospel is announced. It is an event, a decisive moment of sacred history. Christ holds the centre of the stage. 'The eyes of all in the synagogue were fixed on him.' All subsequent authentic preaching will retain something of that event-quality, and its focus of attention will similarly be Jesus Christ. For the Christian preacher is also anointed by

39

the Spirit, and in these last days the Spirit is poured out to make Christ present through the proclamation of his word.

This is part of the notion of proclamation. Christian preaching has an objective quality which saves it from mere demagogy, and also from a spurious evangelism where the preacher lays too much stress on his own alleged personal experience. When the gospel is proclaimed, there is a confrontation which, of its nature, makes demands upon the hearers. Here is something you must do something about. If you come across a road-accident, you either help or walk on: in either case you are committed. Christian preaching announces events, the wonderful works of God in sacred history, particularly the paschal mystery of our Saviour. This very announcing is itself an event. It is a new moment in that sacred history. For it brings the people before a decision of faith. The Lord, who is ever present in mystery in his Church, becomes 'present' to the explicit con-'sciousness of the hearers, and invites them to a new participation in his mystery. This is especially seen in the celebration of the event of the Eucharist. 'For as often as you eat this bread and drink the cup, you proclaim the Lord's death until he comes' (1 Cor 11.26). The rite of the Church itself proclaims through signs and words his paschal mystery, in which we have a present share. The word of the preacher at Mass presents the mystery of Christ under some aspect. The response of faith of the congregation determines the manner and degree of their participation.

In this the Spirit of Christ is also active and present. He does not say his own words, but makes the word of Christ more deeply grasped. This implies a new act of God, a gift of the Spirit. It is not a new revelation. Christ is still the heart of the message. But it means that through the preaching of the word, there is an encounter in faith with the person we know as the Word of God.

The Spirit is at work to achieve this. He acts both in the preacher, if he is faithful, and in the hearers, enabling them to understand and welcome the word of Christ.

Preaching, of course, can also be a non-event. The preacher can abuse his function. He can talk rubbish. Or heresy. The hearer can be ill-disposed to follow the movement of the Spirit. He can fail to give his attention, or his obedience of faith, to the word of God.

St Thomas explains the work of the Holy Spirit in this way. He is speaking of the grace of preaching as a gift of the Spirit which is given for the good of the Church and is superior in power to ordinary human rhetoric. The knowledge anyone has of God, he says, cannot be turned to the advantage of others, except through the medium of speech. And so the Holy Spirit, who provides all the helps that are necessary for the mission of the Church, also assists those who speak in her name. This he does, not only that they should be understood, but also in order that their speech should be effective in the order of grace. This happens in three ways. The preacher speaks,

First, in order to instruct the mind. This happens when someone teaches. Second, in order to move the affections of his hearers, so that they willingly listen to the word of God. This happens when someone pleases his hearers. He should do this not merely to draw attention and honour to himself, but in order that men should be drawn to hear the word of God. Third, in order that people should love what is signified by the words and wish to carry it into practice in their lives. This happens when the hearer becomes obedient. To effect this the Holy Spirit uses the tongue of man as a kind of instrument: but it is he himself who accomplishes the work interiorly (*Summa*, 2a 2ae, q. 177, art. 1, corpus).

St Paul claims that the effectiveness of his preaching depends not so much on his own merely human wisdom, but on the gospel itself of Jesus Christ together with the assistance of the power of the Holy Spirit, both in himself and in his hearers:

I decided to know nothing among you except Jesus Christ and him crucified. And I was with you in weakness and in much fear and trembling; and my speech and my message were not in plausible words of wisdom, but in demonstrations of the Spirit and power, that your faith might not rest in the wisdom of men but in the power of God (1 Cor. 2.2-5).

His preaching imparts the mystery of Christ, 'a secret and hidden wisdom of God', a secret which 'God has revealed to us through the Spirit':

For the Spirit searches everything, even the depths of God... And we impart this in words not taught by human wisdom but taught by the Spirit, interpreting spiritual truths to those who possess the Spirit (1 Cor 2.10,13).

Our Lord promised that the Spirit would guide the disciples 'into all truth' (Jn 16.12). He would help them grasp the word of Christ:

For he will not speak on his own authority, but whatever he hears he will speak, and he will declare to you the things that are to come. He will glorify me, for he will take what is mine and declare it to you. All that the Father has is mine; therefore I said that he will take what is mine and declare it to you (Jn 16.13,14).

Fr Congar explains the work of the Spirit in this way:

The role thus vested in the Holy Spirit is the actualising and interiorising of what Christ said and did... Christ uttered the words of his gospel once; he accomplished our salvation and gave his life, once for all time; he instituted the sacraments and consecrated the apostles once only. Thus did he establish a pattern of life for his people...
A personal appropriation has to be made, not merely by the decision taken by men, which would be neither a principle of unity, nor a principle of divine life, but by a new act of God himself, no longer visibly incarnate at a moment of human history, but giving himself interiorly to each and all. This is the work of the Spirit (Yves M-J. Congar, *Tradition and Traditions*, p. 342; Burns and Oates, London, 1966).

The Holy Spirit, then, is at work both in the preacher and in the hearer. That he will be at work in the Church and her authentic preachers is clear from the account in

Acts where the utterance of the apostles and others is presented as inspired by the same Spirit that inspired the prophets. They derive their mission from Christ and inherit the Spirit he possessed in fulness, especially, as man, in virtue of his resurrection and glorification. The account in Chapter 1 of the ascension evokes the scene where Elijah is taken up into heaven, and Elisha, his successor, inherits a 'double portion of his spirit' because he has been an eye-witness of that event (2 Kings 2). And so 'You shall receive power when the Holy Spirit has come upon you; and you shall be my witnesses in Jerusalem and in all Judea and Samaria and to the end of the earth' (Acts 1.8).

The Apostles spoke with power and confidence. They were aware not only that they had this mission entrusted to them, but also that the Lord would be with them supporting their work. Their authority came from the Lord himself: 'All authority in heaven and on earth has been given to me. Go therefore and make disciples of all nations' (Mt 28.18). But at the same time his going away had meant the gift of the Spirit, which brought them and all humanity into a new relationship with God, indeed, brought them nearer to God. Through the Spirit, the risen Lord would be with them: 'I am with you always, to the close of the age' (Mt 28.20). The long ending of Mark tells us that after the disciples are commanded to 'Go into all the world and preach the gospel to the whole creation,' ...'The Lord Jesus, after he had spoken with them, was taken up into heaven and sat down at the right hand of God. And they went forth and preached everywhere, while the Lord worked with them and confirmed the message by the signs that attended it' (Mk 16.15,19,20).

The apostles were doubly qualified for their mission. They had been with the Lord throughout his preaching life on earth: 'We are witnesses to all that he did both in the country of the Jews and in Jerusalem' (Acts 10.39). They were also the accredited witnesses of his resurrection: 'But God raised him on the third day and made him manifest; not to all the people but to us who were chosen by God as witnesses, who ate and drank with him after he rose from the dead. And he commanded us to preach to the people.' (Acts 10.40-42). Their preaching had what we may call a 'two-way dimension'. Fr E. Schillebeeckx calls it 'horizontal and vertical' (*Revelation and Theology,* pp. 28 ff.). They had a direct experience of their risen Lord, and at the same time they drew on the tradition of the past. The two are not in opposition, since the mystery of Christ is rooted in salvation-history. But their preaching had an immediacy of impact, a here-and-now quality about it. The Lord reigns, Christ is the Lord, it is he who makes his appeal here and now. The apostles' word was Christ's word. This is especially clear in St Paul:

when you received the word of God which you heard from us, you accepted it not as the word of men but as what it really is, the word of God, which is at work in you believers (1 Thess 3.13).
All this is from God, who through Christ reconciled us to himself and gave us the ministry of reconciliation... So we are ambassadors for Christ, God making his appeal through us (2 Cor 5.18,20).

At the same time, the apostles were not just ecstatics with a purely personal vision to communicate. The explanation of the great events they proclaimed required reference back to the way God himself had prepared the minds of his People. There was an objective pedagogy to be followed.

Our Lord himself uses it. The two disciples who were scandalized by the events of Good Friday took the road away from the community at Jerusalem. Our Lord appears. He is present at their side, yet he is not present 'to' them. They do not understand or believe in his saving death and resurrection. And so they do not recognize him. His presence means nothing to them. Their eyes are 'held'. Our Lord begins to teach them. The Word turns to the word, an image of the Church in all her preaching office. The Spirit makes their hearts burn within them, and the risen Lord, using the educative word in history, becomes present to their faith. They finally recognize him in the breaking of bread and return to enter the communion of love at Jerusalem:

And he said to them: 'O foolish and slow of heart to believe all that the prophets had spoken! Was it not necessary that the Christ should suffer these things and enter his glory? And beginning with Moses and all the prophets, he interpreted to them in all the scriptures the things concerning himself (Lk 24.25-27).

He does the same to the apostles in Jerusalem (Lk 24.44,45). Philip the deacon explains the text of Isaiah to the eunuch: 'and beginning with this scripture he told him the good news of Jesus' (Acts 8.35).

Not all preachers, of course, have the special gifts of the apostles. Their preaching was a part of the foundation of the Church in its actual coming into being. It became a constituent element of the deposit of revelation. But in his own way, every preacher, clerical or lay, has a share in the Spirit that descended on the Church at Pentecost and is still active in the Church where Christ is ever present in mystery and through the activity of the Spirit is made present to the faith of succeeding generations.

An early Christian text, the *Didache,* speaks of the reverence due to the preacher if he is faithful to his mission:

My child, be mindful day and night of him who speaks the word of God to you. You are to honour him as you would the Lord. For where the Lordship (of God) is proclaimed, the Lord is present (*Didache,* 4.1).

CHAPTER VI

THE STAGES OF PREACHING

A complaint regularly heard today about preaching is that it is not practical. People often feel that what they hear from the pulpit is not relevant to their lives. It makes no impact.

No doubt the complaint is often justified. It is easy for preachers to slip into generalities and pious platitudes, especially when they have not prepared the sermon well. They can repeat worn-out phrases or fall back on their own hobby-horses. However, the necessary messages do not arise exclusively out of the consideration of one's personal problems and range of vision. Such an approach can easily turn round in circles upon itself. At some point reference has to be made to revelation, the word of God at source. It is in the light of meditation on the word that situations can be clarified and proper direction given. Judgment is required and discernment of the promptings of the Holy Spirit.

At the same time, the preacher must take account of the condition and mentality of the people he is addressing. Such consideration is necessary both at the community or social level, and also at the individual level. The word of God grew and took root in Hebrew soil. We can see in the New Testament how the approach of St Matthew, who was preaching to the Jews, differs from the approach of St Luke, who had the gentile audience more in view. St John too has a good eye on those Docetists who said the Lord's body was not real but an illusion. Missionary preaching in particular has to study carefully the mentalities it is dealing with.

Critics of the modern catechetical movement are often unaware of the extent to which it stresses the need for careful appraisal of the person or persons to whom the message is addressed. They may hear of stressing the Bible, the liturgy, the kerygma of the apostles, the history of salvation, but may feel these approaches are not 'practical' for the people they are dealing with, whether it be rowdy adolescents on a sleepy afternoon, or a complacent congregation happy with the so-called traditional Catholic devotions. But in fact modern institutes of pastoral and catechetical training will have courses on religious psychology, where important scientific studies of human maturity are related to the growth of maturity in faith. Also modern sociology has a great deal to say about the functioning of groups of any kind, much of which is directly relevant to community structures in the Church.

The Second Vatican Council was aware of the need. The *Decree on the Ministry of Priests* says:

No doubt, priestly preaching is often very difficult in the circumstances of the modern world. If it is to influence the mind of the listener more fruitfully, such preaching must not present God's Word in a general and abstract fashion only, but it must apply the perennial truth of the gospel to the concrete circumstances of life (*Ministry of Priests*, n. 4).

The *Decree on the Training of Priests* urges careful study of the sources of revelation and sound theology in order that priests may have something of value to say about contemporary problems:

Let them learn to search for solutions to human problems with the light of revelation, to apply eternal truths to the changing conditions of human affairs, and to communicate such truths in a manner suited to contemporary man (*Priestly Formation*, n. 16).

The *Pastoral Constitution on the Church in the Modern World* is most definite that theology is not enough. Theologians themselves, and especially those engaged in the ministry of the word, must give attention to the knowledge of man and society that has been gained from objective scientific investigation over the years:

While adhering to the methods and requirements proper to theology, theologians are invited to seek continually for more suitable ways of communicating doctrine to the men of their times. For the deposit of faith or revealed truths are one thing; the manner in which they are formulated without violence to their meaning and significance is another.

In pastoral care, appropriate use must be made not only of theological principles, but also of the findings of the secular sciences, especially of psychology and sociology. Thus the faithful can be brought to live the faith in a more thorough and mature way (n. 62).

Preaching, in fact, must aim at the conversion of the whole man, and it must therefore take account of his whole personality-development and include a reference to his situation in life and in contemporary society. This is particularly necessary when dealing with prospective converts. Before the word can gain an entry to the mind, a considerable amount of preparatory work may be necessary. The soil has to be prepared for the seed of the word. Otherwise it may simply encounter prejudice. It has been the practice, for instance, to begin to 'catechize' people, in the sense of teaching the ideas in a catechism of doctrine, before they are really prepared to accept the fundamentals of faith. It is generally recognized now that positive doctrinal instruction, or even biblical-historical instruction is useless unless the ground is first prepared. An important theological point is involved. The question is: does the person have faith at least in a global sense of accepting God and Jesus Christ and the Church? This may not be easy to determine in practice, but in principle the distinction should be clear, for it has a fundamental importance for method.

The first stage of faith, in the proper sense, involves a surrender and a commitment. The 'obedience of faith' is there. Converts wish to join the Christian community and ask to be instructed. If they have reached that stage, then the process of preaching will be able to use the sources of the word of God, because the person has already accepted the authority of these sources and of the Church which preaches them. His faith is built up in this way. Thus the starting-point for instruction is the already-existing faith of this catechumen who is already committed to seeking baptism in the Church (or admission to communion with it).

But if we are dealing with an enquirer who is at a stage where he is being prompted by God's grace to turn towards the Church and has not yet arrived at a stage of commitment, then, in principle, the starting-point is not faith. Rather, faith is the end-product, so to speak, of this form of preaching. There will not be much use speaking about the Church's sacramental system, if he is not yet sure if he believes in God.

There are three stages of the development of faith to which correspond three types of preaching. These differ both as to content and manner. They are usually called pre-evangelization, evangelization, and catechesis. Some would add the stage of homiletic preaching at liturgical celebration, where, in principle, a well-instructed and mature congregation is present. The aim of evangelization is to produce the basic conversion, i.e. the first acceptance of the gospel, including the Church. This is also referred to as the stage of 'kerygma', after the basic short summaries of the gospel found in the New Testament. Pre-evangelization includes everything that can be done to lead the prospective convert to the *openness* (not yet *acceptance*), needed for evangelization. The stage that follows evangelization is, according to many writers, the stage of catechesis in the strict sense, where already existing faith is built up.

We have then the following scheme:

a. Pre-evangelization;
b. Evangelization (or kerygma);
c. Catechesis;
d. Homily.

It would be unwise to conceive these divisions as representing water-tight compartments. A homily can obviously have a catechetical element, and usually has to some extent. One can in the first stage light a few evangelical fuses, hoping they may go off. In practice, with any individual, it may be difficult to discern just what is going on in his soul, but the distinctions should provide teacher or preacher with some useful guide-lines. It should also be noted that these terms are not always used in the same way in different countries, and that over the last few years there has been some development of thought on their precise significance. The term catechesis, in particular, is often used to mean any kind of religious teaching.

A full discussion of these terms would require several treatises on their own. Here I shall select a few points about each in order to clarify the way they are distinguished in general.

a. Pre-evangelization

Often referred to as the 'preambles to faith', this process used to be conceived perhaps too exclusively in intellectual terms. Arguments turned on the relationship of faith and reason. Apologetics tended to be very rationalistic, with proofs lined up like a course in geometry. The main point here would seem to be to take the person as he is and start from his present attitudes and ideas. This can work in a negative and a positive sense. Wrong ideas have to be cleared up. Intellectual difficulties have to be solved. But, also, account must be taken of the person's feelings and values, his attachment to the society he is living in, his whole social and cultural milieu. The obstacles have to be overcome that prevent him having a real encounter with the word of the gospel, that obstruct his view so that he is not really challenged. How many people live side-by-side with Christians, and yet never feel their own values seriously questioned? It is not that the gospel message is not powerful: it is simply not heard. Nor would it be of any particular use to thrust it unwanted on unprepared ears. That in itself would be a lack of respect for the people we are dealing with, who are entitled to respect for honestly-held views. Only a crude form of evangelism thrusts itself on everybody indiscriminately. It tends to do more harm than good.

More positively, pre-evangelization can try to build on the real values the person already possesses, and which can find a fulfilment and even fuller expression in Christianity. The sincere communist, for instance, can have a strongly developed sense of social justice, which, we hope, may be readily baptised.

In all this there must be a respect for the person. In Fr Nebreda's phrase, we must speak 'to' him, and not 'at' him (*Distinguishing the Different Stages of Missionary Preaching,* Alfonso Nebreda, S.J., Rome, 1962).

b. Evangelization

This term can in fact be used in two ways. First, in the sense of that preaching which aims at bringing the prospective convert's spiritual education to the point at which he is ready to make the basic decision of faith. It is discussed whether or no this necessarily involves a rather violent period, or shock, when he must break loose from his former way of life and sense of security. Certainly many converts have an experience something like this. Others maintain that a gradual acceptance of the faith is possible, and the way can be smooth. But the preacher or catechist will have the delicate task of discerning when in fact the convert is ready, and ought to face the decision.

The other application of the term concerns preaching in general and any form of religious teaching. Even adult Catholics in a sense require constant 'conversion'. Not that they have lost the faith, but that it is always necessary to reaffirm our 'fundamental option' for God in our lives. Then there are those who have never really grown up in their faith, and live with the mental structures and religious attitudes they had as young children. We are always complaining of inadequately-instructed adult Catholics. Often it is not instruction they need so much as evangelization. They really need to be re-converted in a quite fundamental way. The same is also true of many school children whose parents are weak Catholics. They may never at any stage make a real act of faith, and a great deal of the formal catechesis they receive is simply projected on stony ground.

c. Catechesis

In the New Testament scholars recognize a distinction between the first announcing of gospel (the apostolic kerygma), and subsequent instruction, both moral and doctrinal, for which the terms *didache* or *didascalia* are used. Many modern writers use the term 'catechesis' to describe this further stage of the building-up of faith, or at least see the catechetical function as primarily concerned with it.

This means that what we have normally considered as a purely instructional function, in the sense of 'learning your catechism', must have much more of a religious content in the sense of a development of a religious response of faith. Formerly, catechetical instruction could confine itself to instructing the mind. The religious life of the community, the home, the parish, the milieu, supported the life of faith in the community. In our modern secularized society this is no longer so; rather the contrary. The Catholic teacher, then, must take on much more the functions of a preacher of the word of God, and both evangelize and catechize.

On this basis, then, we can specify that catechesis should have the following three elements: it should instruct, it should form, it should introduce to a personal relationship with God.

Instruction will always be necessary and should never be lost sight of. The move against the old emphasis on abstract doctrinal ideas does not mean that the needs of the developing intelligence should not be met. If they are not met, there is danger of immaturity in faith, or subsequent rejection if religious ideas bear the stamp of childhood or adolescence. Throughout adult life, this restructuring is necessary. Faith comes by hearing and grows by hearing, and this hearing comes from the word of God, which is inexhaustible. It is also meaningful.

Instruction is, however, not the only aim. The whole human personality must grow towards a Christian maturity, and that will involve a whole mentality, a set of values adopted and habitually acted upon. The whole affective and emotional pattern directly affects religious response and life. Preachers and teachers must aim to form the whole man. For religion is particularly at the mercy of disorderly tendencies deeply-rooted in the emotional and affective life of man as he develops. A defective religious education can result in a crop of superstitious attitudes, magical tendencies, taboos, anxious fears. They can pass under the guise of piety and devotion.

Finally, catechesis should bring the subject before God himself through the mediation of his word. That is why the modern catechetical movement uses the Bible, the liturgy, doctrine, the life of the Church, as its main sources. For these are the sources of the word of God, and through them God becomes present to the active faith of the person catechized.

These three aims are always present in catechesis. But it is the third that is its main task.

d. Homily

This term usually refers to a familiar discourse on a text of scripture together with a practical application to life. It tends to be used more widely now for preaching at Mass or at any other liturgical celebration. Since the Second Vatican Council interest in the sermon at Mass has increased, and it is becoming agreed that the context of preaching within the liturgy makes certain demands.

For the purposes of explaining the function of the liturgical homily as one of the stages of preaching outlined in this chapter, it is enough to say that it assumes a well-instructed congregation who are already evangelized and catechized. The homily, therefore, can aim at an ever-deepening faith in a mature way, with an application to participation in the particular liturgical action with which it is associated.

The *Liturgy Constitution* says that the homily should draw its content mainly from 'scriptural and liturgical sources' (*Liturgy*, n. 35). It should proclaim the wonderful works of God in the history of salvation, 'that is, the mystery of Christ, which is ever made present within us, especially in the celebration of the liturgy' *(ibid.)*. This gives the homily at Mass a special character. It has a double term of reference: the scriptural readings that are the basis of the liturgy of the Word, and the eucharistic action. It proclaims the word that has been read, in which the mystery of Christ is announced, and it aims at enabling those present to share in the mystery of Christ made present especially in the liturgy. The word of the readings and homily is realized, actualized in the sacramental celebration and presence, a presence which is not only objective and 'real', but also, through the preaching of the word, subjective and personal. Indeed corporate and communal. For the word that is preached at Mass or at any other liturgical gathering, 'assembles' the people. They are not an assembly simply by reason of the fact that they all happen to be in the same place at the same time. They are in communion in faith and in the gift of the Spirit of Christ. The Word is an invitation to explicit faith and communion, with Christ and with one another. This is 'realized' in the memorial sacrifice, in which they also participate as a community. The homily, then, cannot be separated from this mystery of communion and assembly which is the manifestation of the abiding presence of Christ in his sacrament of unity, the Church.

But it means that the homily should be relevant to its theological context. A merely moralistic sermon would not normally be enough, nor even a merely doctrinal sermon. What is regularly required is a liturgical sermon, which applies the word of the liturgy to the faith of the congregation and thereby contributes to 'creating' the liturgical assembly here and now, just as the word fundamentally established the assembly of the people of God when they were first called to faith. The Mass rite is itself a 'word' whereby God still speaks to his people and affirms his new covenant. The liturgy of the word, with its homily, is a kind of 'fore-word' to the eternal Word of God that is uttered, with its promise, at the high point of the Church's self-consciousness and prayer.

In actual fact and practice, the homily has to take account of the real state of the congregation. Sinners are to be converted. The ill-instructed require further catechesis. Very rarely can one assume familiarity with the Old Testament. This creates a special problem. Ideally, instruction should also be carried out at other times and in other places. In fact, the Sunday Mass is the only time when large numbers come into contact with the teaching Church. The homily therefore has to be adapted to the needs of the congregation:

In the Christian community itself, especially among those who seem to understand or believe little of what they practise, the

55

preaching of the word is needed for the very administration of the sacraments. For these are sacraments of faith, and faith is born of the Word and nourished by it (*Ministry of Priests*, n. 4).

In the normal parish situation the preacher has certain advantages and disadvantages. In the first place, he usually knows his congregation better than the visiting preacher. Secondly, from the fact that he is preaching regularly, he can provide instruction based on some system, and there can be continuity. He can emphasize certain points over a period. Just what system should be used is much disputed. Ideally the scripture readings and the liturgical year should provide the necessary basis, both having their focus on the mystery of Christ in his paschal mystery. Sermon programmes used to be issued by diocesan authorities that were based on the classic treatises of dogma and moral, and often led to the absurd situation where one might be preaching on the laws of marriage on an important liturgical feast. A disadvantage is that the people hear the same voice all the time. This is not insurmountable in principle, if the priest is giving an appropriate amount of his time to reading and meditation on the sources of the word and in particular to studying the current developments in the Church, of which, in all conscience, there is enough to be done and said.

The homily at Mass, then, has to be at once practical, taking into account the condition of the congregation, but it also has to follow the laws of its special context. There is need too, for homiletic preaching in the course of the administration of the other sacraments, for the same principles apply to the awakening of an enlightened faith for fruitful participation.

CHAPTER VII

THE SOURCES OF THE WORD TODAY

Through the 'service of the word', the message of Christ reaches men in all ages. The question arises: how do we come into contact with the word of God today?

The general answer is: in the Church who is 'equipped with the gifts of her founder' (*The Church*, n. 5). She has many ministries and many sacred activities. To some of her members are assigned in a special way the ministry of the word for the benefit and service of the people: bishops, priests, deacons, approved catechists and teachers. But it is the Church herself who is the first preacher, because the Church is Christ and Christ is the Word, and his light shines through the life of the Church in all its variety.

To say this is not to say that we cannot also find illumination for our faith in sources which we normally think of as 'outside the Church'. God can speak to man in many ways, though the word of revelation in Christ remains the foundation of Christian faith and the principle of unity in the human race. For instance, separated Christian bodies, who are related to the Church by the special bond of baptism, and in whom the Holy Spirit is at work, are for the Catholic a constant source of edification and enlightenment in his faith. Secular society has its values from which we constantly learn. Non-christian religions too have much to offer. In the very 'signs of the times', in the social and political situations that arise, we may hope to discern the hand of God and his will for us.

But it is principally in his word in the Church, in her institutions and her ministries, that God speaks to us today. No doubt there are many possible schemes whereby we can say, 'This is how the Church preaches today', but for convenience we can say there are four principal sources of the word:

a. The witness of the life of the Church;
b. The Bible;
c. The liturgy;
d. The doctrinal pronouncements of the teaching authority.

a. The Witness of the life of the Church

Not so long ago, catechetical writers would have said that there are three main sources of the teaching and preaching, three main 'ways' in which God speaks to us, and therefore three main ways we should use as the basis of teaching in pulpit or classroom. The three ways were: the Bible, the liturgy, doctrine. At that time the emphasis on the Bible and the liturgy was relatively new and something of a break-through. Today, a fourth is added: 'the witness of the life of the Church'. (In fact, the Council adds a fifth: the teaching of the Fathers of the Church, as a special source of her living tradition.) No doubt teachers and preachers always did use this fourth source. The example of the lives of the Saints has never been absent in practice from the Church's proclamation, though these lives have not always been preached in an authentic manner. Some books on the saints and some statues in our churches were better suppressed.

But the life of the Church itself is a sign for faith, a sign of God's presence and action by which he speaks to our faith. The First Vatican Council was very definite about this, and in the Second the document on the Church begins with a reference to Christ the Light of the world, and takes this phrase, *Lumen Gentium,* for its title. In particular, witness of the Christian lives of her members is a manifestation of the work of God in the world, a true 'word of God' that convicts the world of sin and shows forth the face of Christ in the world.

58

For children, the concrete witness of the lives of their parents is their first and best introduction to the faith. In their parents, 'the first preachers', they see the faith alive and in the flesh, and it obviously belongs to the present, not the past. So the word is present to them.

Like the Church at Corinth, the People of God today should be easily readable and bear their witness. St Paul says of the witness of his Corinthians:

You yourselves are our letter of recommendation, written on your hearts, to be known and read by all men; and you show that you are a letter from Christ delivered by us, written not with ink, but with the Spirit of God, not on tablets of stone but on tablets of human hearts (1 Cor 3.2).

We may find it strange to think of this kind of witness as a form of the word of God, but it is the language of the Council. Sometimes it uses connected words, like 'revelation' or 'light', but the sense is the same. For instance, religious by their lives should be a sign of the mystery of Christ present in the Church. Each order or congregation will reveal some aspect of the life of Christ:

Religious should carefully consider that through them, to believers and non-believers alike, the Church truly wishes to give an increasingly clearer revelation of Christ. Through them, Christ should be shown contemplating on the mountain, announcing God's kingdom to the multitude... (*The Church*, n. 46).

This witness is not a kind of charade or mime. It is the Church revealing Christ. This word of God really introduces men to faith and personal contact with God, as experience shows. The Council is even more explicit when it speaks of the lives of the Saints of the Church:

In the lives of those who shared our humanity and yet were transformed into especially successful images of Christ (2 Cor 3.18), God vividly manifests to men his presence and his face. He speaks to us in them, and gives us a sign of his kingdom, to which we are powerfully drawn, surrounded as we are by so many witnesses (Heb 12.1), and having such an argument for the truth of the gospel (*The Church*, n. 50).

The Liturgy Constitution adds the specific reference that the celebration of the feast-days of the saints is a preaching of the paschal mystery, which the Church thus 'proclaims'.

The community life of the Church itself is a specific form of witness, since it manifests the charity of Christ. This point is especially developed in the texts dealing with catechumens. Priests are to remember that their pastoral efforts are not directed towards people as individuals only, but that an essential part of their office is to build communities. Such active Christian communities may then function as living witnesses to the gospel and draw men to Christ:

Moreover, by charity, prayer, example, and works of penance, the Church community exercises a true motherhood towards souls who are to be led to Christ. For this community constitutes an effective instrument by which the path to Christ and to his Church is pointed out and made smooth for unbelievers, and by which the faithful are aroused, nourished and strengthened for spiritual combat (*Ministry of Priests*, n. 6).

These are a few examples of the way in which the Church preaches through the lives of her members. They are forms of existential witness, effective in themselves as showing the Holy Spirit at work in the Church. They can also be made the object of explicit comment by the word of the preacher or catechist, who can point to their significance, as did the prophets of old with the wonderful works of God, and so present this witness effectively for the edification of their hearers.

b. The scriptures

Among the sources of the word of God, the written text of the scriptures holds the primary place. In a special and unique sense they are God's word because they are inspired:

For, inspired by God and committed once and for all to writing, they impart the word of God himself without change, and make the voice of the Holy Spirit resound in the words of the prophets and apostles. Therefore, like the Christian religion itself, all the preaching of the Church must be nourished and ruled by sacred scripture (*Revelation*, n. 21).

For this reason the word of God in scripture, along with the tradition that guards and interprets it, will always be the 'primary and perpetual foundation' both of theology and of all forms of the ministry of the word.

For the sacred Scriptures contain the word of God and, since they are inspired, really are the word of God... By the same word of scripture the ministry of the word also takes wholesome nourishment and yields fruits of holiness...
This ministry includes pastoral preaching, catechetics, and all other Christian instruction, among which the liturgical homily should have an exceptional place (*Revelation*, n. 24).

The Council not only urges every preacher and teacher to become familiar with the word of God in Scripture, lest any become 'an empty preacher of the word of God outwardly, who is not a listener to it inwardly,' but also urges all the faithful to take up the reading of the scriptures and prayerful meditation upon them, a meditation which is necessary if the word is to be savoured and appreciated in any depth. The reason given is simply this: 'ignorance of the scriptures is ignorance of Christ'. 'Therefore they should gladly put themselves in touch with the sacred text itself, whether it be through the liturgy, rich in the divine word, or through devotional reading, or through instruction etc.' (n. 25).

Many Catholics are still afraid of the scriptures, especially the Old Testament. Many homes do not possess a copy of the whole Bible. If they do, it is a fair guess that in most cases it is opened rarely. The Catholic laity are not particularly to be blamed for this state of affairs. The history of the counter-reformation has probably a lot to do with it. They have received little encouragement from their priests, and the priests, in their turn, in many cases did not receive sufficient guidance in their seminary days. On the contrary, many may well have been put off by what they were given, and come away with the feeling that everything is difficult. The *Constitution on Divine Revelation* recommends a more pastoral approach to those who design seminary courses, and the reforms are under way in many places (*Revelation*, n. 23).

The same Constitution ends with the words:

Just as the life of the Church grows through persistent participation in the Eucharistic mystery, so we may hope for a new surge of spiritual vitality from intensified veneration for God's word, which 'lasts for ever' (Is 40.8; 1 Pet 1.23-25).

It is an ancient tradition in the Church to regard the word of scripture as food for the soul and to place it on the same level as the bread of life in the Eucharist. The Council in this text indicates the way to a restoration of this mentality in Catholic practice and devotion. Already in the book of Deuteronomy we read: 'that he might make you know that man does not live by bread alone but that man lives by everything that proceeds out of the mouth of the Lord' (Deut 8.3). St Augustine bids us think of the food of our souls in the Eucharist and the word of God when we pray the Our Father: 'give us this day our daily bread'. Origen tells us we partake of the blood of Christ when we hear the scriptures just as we do in communion: 'we drink the blood of Christ not only in the sacramental rite, but also when we receive his word, in which life consists, as he himself has said: "The words which I have spoken to you are spirit and life" ' (*In Num. Hom.* 16.9). Origen also requires an examination of conscience in the preacher before he ascends the pulpit, on a parallel with his preparation for celebrating the Eucharist. A later writer, probably Caesarius of Arles (d. 542) writes as follows:

I have a question to ask you, brothers and sisters. Tell me, which do you consider to be of greater value: the word of God, or the body of Christ? If you wish to answer correctly, you would have to say that the word of God is not to be treated as inferior to the body of Christ. How careful we are that nothing slip from our hand and fall to the floor. But the same care must be taken to ensure that the word of God, which has been given into our keeping, is never lost to our hearts through our thinking and speaking of other things. The one who is negligent in hearing the word of God is no less guilty than the one who, through carelessness, allows the body of Christ to fall to the floor (Sermon 78.2).

The tradition appears again in the *Imitation of Christ* of Thomas à Kempis (d. 1471). He speaks of two tables on the sanctuary:

The one is the table of the altar, on which rests the holy bread, the body of Christ; the other holds the true faith and leads us surely behind the veil to the holy of holies (4.11).

Finally, we read in the *Constitution on Divine Revelation*:

The Church has always venerated the divine scriptures just as she venerates the body of the Lord, since from the table both of the word of God and of the body of Christ she unceasingly receives and offers to the faithful the bread of life, especially in the sacred liturgy (n. 21).

We might notice that the Council does not speak of two tables, but of one table from which we receive the bread of life both in the form of the word and of the sacrament. This precision significantly points to their unity and mutual interdependence. For it is the same Lord who gives himself through his word and through the sacrament, and our communion in faith and love relies on both together.

In spite of the recommendation of scripture in all the sources, many people still feel that the world of scripture, particularly the Old Testament, is too remote from the world we live in today. A housewife once said to me: 'Jeroboam? what's he got to do with me and my five kids and my difficult husband?' The difficulty is a real one, for the scriptures were written at a certain time in history for people who not only used a different language from ours, but whose whole cast of mind, culture, and history were different.

One school of thought would push through a radical re-writing, or 'demythologizing'. The proposal is that we should strip the scripture down to its hard core of content and restate it in modern terms. Teachers and preachers are always in fact engaged in presenting the scriptural message in their own words in some way, and applying it to their hearers. But given that the scripture had God for its author, we shall always have the task of leading people to contact with the text itself. We have the same problem of adaptation and relevance with liturgical texts and gestures that use scriptural language, symbol, and allusion. Some would wish to get rid of these altogether and present us with a kind of kitchen-sink liturgy. For the moment, at any rate, the Council sees scriptural education as 'of paramount importance' for the celebration of the liturgy, and this represents a decision of policy. Many have objected to what they consider to be irrelevant scriptural symbolism. They say symbols cannot be learned. They have to come from ordinary life, naturally. Otherwise everything is artificial and also superficial. The point, of course, is of particular validity on the missions where worship has to be closely related to indigenous culture.

However the problem of adaptation to modern mentalities be solved, liturgical worship can never wholly be divorced from its roots in scripture. Liturgical signs derive their meaning from scripture not only in the sense that they use its language, e.g. oil, water, light, but also in the sense that they derive their meaning from the history of salvation of which scripture is a record. The liturgy, indeed, is its continuation and actualization. Bible and liturgy cannot be separated. The liturgy, in the sense of its essential meaning, is unintelligible without the Bible. Are we to separate the Mass from the Last Supper? Can we understand the Last Supper without some reference to the history of the people of Israel? The form may be adapted to a certain extent, but the historical reality, the continuity in the mystery of Christ, remains, and can only be grasped in depth in the light of education in faith from the word of God as it has appeared in history.

The Bible need not be so remote. So much of it is concerned with man's basic needs and feelings, his situation before God and the great and ultimate problems of life. This much we have in common. But we also need faith in the Bible. It carries the mystery of God's presence which he has attached to his word in this form. It has application in every age. It lasts for ever (1 Pet 1.23-25).

c. The Liturgy

'Going to Mass' has for so long been associated in the minds of the people with a duty and a 'commandment of the Church', that it is difficult for them to appreciate the many rich insights that the modern liturgical movement has produced. A major work of catechesis is required, not only in the general theological principles that underly the form in which the Church's prayer is expressed, but also, in detail, of the rites and signs which it uses. 'Instruction which is more explicitly liturgical should also be imparted in a variety of ways' (*Liturgy*, n. 35). The text goes on to add that this should be done in the course of the ceremony if necessary.

These rites are to be intelligible. 'They should be within the people's powers of comprehension, and normally should not require much explanation' (*ibid.* n. 34). They are to be reformed: 'so that they express more clearly the holy things they signify. Christian people, as far as possible, should be able to understand them with ease and to take part in them fully, actively, and as befits a community' (*ibid*. n. 21).

In order that the people may understand them, the Council lays a serious duty on priests to promote the liturgical instruction of their people: 'With zeal and patience, pastors of souls must promote the liturgical instruction of the faithful, and also their active participation in the liturgy both internally and externally' (*ibid*. n. 19). For this intelligent and active participation is 'the primary and indispensable source from which the faithful are to derive the true Christian spirit. Therefore, through the needed programme of instruction, pastors of souls must zealously strive to achieve it in all their pastoral work' (*ibid*. n. 14).

There are many reasons why participation in the liturgy is 'the primary and indispensable source from which the faithful are to derive the true Christian spirit'. The assembly of the Church is a special situation endowed, in the providence of God, with a special promise and blessing. Christ is always present in his Church, but 'especially in her liturgical celebrations' (*ibid*. n. 7). As noted in the section on the Divine Office, the liturgy, at which the Church prays, is 'the very prayer which Christ himself, together with his body, addresses to the Father' (*ibid*. n. 84). The assembly of the Church creates what we might call the 'event-situation'. In a way not ordinarily given in any other situation, Christ may be 'present' to the faith of the people. For this, their faith must be active, and the liturgical structures and ministries, the external forms and rites, constitute a preaching of the Church to her people within which the word of God is addressed to them for their active and fruitful response. 'For in the liturgy, God speaks to his people and Christ is still proclaiming his gospel. And the people reply to God by both song and prayer' (*ibid*. n. 33).

Because in the liturgy, 'the work of our redemption is

exercised', it is 'the outstanding means by which the faithful can express in their lives, and manifest to others, the mystery of Christ and the real nature of the true Church' (*ibid*. n. 2). If the word is adequately presented to the faithful, and they respond in faith, they come not only to know the presence of Christ, but also to participate in the actual accomplishment here and now of his paschal mystery. The liturgical assembly is endowed with these properties. 'Because it is an action of Christ the priest and of his Body, the Church, it is a sacred action surpassing all others. No other action of the Church can match its claim to efficacy, nor equal the degree of it' (*ibid*. n. 7).

The liturgy of the word is itself designed to activate this response. 'He is present in his word, since it is he himself who speaks when the holy scriptures are read in the Church' (*ibid*. n. 7). The primary function of the liturgical homily is to break this bread of the word for the nourishment of the assembly who are to be led to more fruitful, more nourishing participation in the sacrament as a united people. For just as they are assembled by the word, so too the word of the sacrament, the sign and gesture by which the New Covenant is reaffirmed between God and man, establishes, ratifies and cements their union in the love of God and of one another. The end of all preaching is charity, and whereas normally the People of God are dispersed about town and country pursuing their work-a-day tasks so that their basic unity in the Spirit is not clearly to be seen, in the liturgical assembly they come together and their unity in the Spirit is made manifest. Thus the fundamental word in the Church, the word that is Christ, shines forth. This mystery the Church preaches, teaches, reveals, proclaims and makes known by her communal action we call the liturgy.

It is not only in the reading of the scriptures and the word of the homily that she preaches. The sacramental signs are themselves words of God. For 'the visible signs used by the liturgy to signify invisible divine things have been chosen by Christ or the Church' (*ibid*. n. 33). In them Christ is especially active and his presence is revealed. They accomplish what they signify. The basic significance of each sacrament is surrounded by prayer, rites and gestures by which the Church expresses what she believes about them and what she is doing in them. Since the sacraments are sacraments of faith this expression is a form of preaching addressed to the participants. Hence the necessity that they should understand them, and be well instructed in them. For these signs are pregnant with meaning. They express divine, invisible things, often in a brief but very 'dense' way. The participant has to have his perceptions sharpened by prior preaching or catechesis if he is to enter fully into the liturgical action. The minister, too, must be conscious of this preaching function of the rite. He must bear in mind that what he says and does is meant to be followed prayerfully by his congregation, and he must give them time to assimilate what is pronounced and proclaimed. For 'when the Church prays or sings or acts, the faith of those taking part is nourished and their minds raised to God, so that they may offer him the worship which reason requires and more copiously receive his grace' (*ibid*. n. 33).

The liturgy 'contains abundant instruction for the faithful' (*ibid*. n. 33). But it will not do this effectively unless the people are well-prepared, and this lays a serious duty on priests and catechists. Religious education in schools, catechetical initiatives in parishes must have this participation as a basic aim. Without it, the word of God in the liturgy is not heard, as experience has unhappily shown. The liturgical situation has obvious advantages from a catechetical point of view. There is a sacred atmosphere. So much religious teaching struggles against odds because this basic requirement is absent. We 'learn by doing', and in the liturgy we have an experience of the reality of the Church in which we participate. A good catechesis, we are told, should end in some form of commitment in faith. In the liturgy, the opportunity is there in participation in the sacraments, for this is a 'sacred action surpassing all others' (*ibid.* n. 7). Finally, because it is the prayer of the Church, it expresses her faith. It is 'objective'. It preserves us from the imbalances to which purely personal and private forms of devotion are exposed. Its centre and heart is the mystery of Christ, who leads us to the Father in the unity of the Holy Spirit.

d. The doctrinal pronouncements of the teaching authority

Since the teaching authority of the Church is treated in detail elsewhere in this series, I shall not dwell at length upon it here. But clearly the developing understanding of the word of revelation as it is expressed in the official doctrinal pronouncements of the Church provides a guide for the preacher and teacher. In particular the work of the ecumenical councils demands his attention. This is especially necessary in our day, when a serious and radical attempt has been made to renew the spiritual life of the People of God. The Second Vatican Council was in the main a pastoral council, that is to say, one concerned with the building up of the people in faith. Here too, the preacher must listen to the voice of the Holy Spirit, without which his preaching will be robbed of its contemporary relevance and therefore of its efficacy. God still speaks in his Church in many ways, and one of those ways is through the voice of the assembled College of bishops, united under the authority of the Pope, in whom the voices of Peter and the apostles come to us in a way that is designed to meet the urgent needs of our day.

CHAPTER VIII

WHO PREACHES? I. THE LAITY

In our day so many people are dissatisfied with the state of preaching from the pulpit, that they question whether the priest should do it at all. The malaise has perhaps been felt by priests themselves, since they clearly have not been doing as much of it as they should, nor giving it sufficient priority in their time and effort. The Vatican Council has laid down rules obliging priests to preach at Mass on Sundays and holydays of obligation, and strongly urged preaching a homily at other Masses. This kind of legislation reflects a general state of disinterest and neglect. Otherwise the strictures would not be necessary. It cannot be doubted that many people do not look to the priest for their enlightenment and instruction on the faith.

Father Godin of Lumen Vitae in one of his books records a saying of François Mauriac. The writer had been asked what he looked for in a priest and he replied:

The priest is the man who first gives me forgiveness and then places the host in my mouth (Quoted in *Le Dieu des Enfants et le Dieu des Parents*; Casterman, Brussels, 1963, p. 47).

He then went on to say that the priest should give him God and not speak about him.

The attitude is quite common. A priest is someone who dispenses grace. He has the powers which can make people holy. He is a kind of sacred mechanic. He has the devices, the tools. He knows the switches and how to operate them for us. We are no more interested in his ideas than in those of the man who drives our bus. An exception might be that he can remind us of the rules and obligations we live under. He is a kind of divine delivery-man. And a policeman too. 'Preaching?', said one distinguished layman. 'Useless. What can a priest tell a layman? He doesn't live his kind of life. He doesn't have his experience. Why should he presume to stand up there in the pulpit and tell us what to do? He knows nothing about it.'

A learned lady once said to me: 'All we want of priests is that they administer the sacraments to us. That is what they are there for. I do not look for my education from priests. They baptize us when we are children, they give us absolution when we have sinned, they say Mass for us, and when we are sick and dying they come and administer the last rites. I do not expect them to teach me anything.'

This mentality is at the opposite pole from the Reformers' view of the ministry in the sixteenth century. They were concerned to show that the only function of the ministry was the preaching function, and that if a man did not perform this task, he could not be described as a minister of religion. It is interesting to see how far to the opposite extreme so many Catholics (and priests) have swung. The view is quite common that the sacrament of orders gives certain powers in the administration of the sacraments, but nothing in the way of capacity for preaching. This is conceived usually as an accident of training, or merely a matter of delegation from the bishop.

A variant of the attitude, though not so overt, is found when people urge that the priest should not have the exclusive use of the air at Mass. The pews should be allowed to speak back, not only at home over the dinner-table, but there and then in the church.

The answer to this is complex, and indeed takes us into the next two chapters. It involves the whole question of the mission of the laity to preach the gospel and how that is to be understood. I shall deal with that question first, and then go on to discuss the preaching function of the hierarchical priesthood.

First, let it be said, there is no particular theological objection to laymen preaching in some form or other, even at Mass and other liturgical functions. There may be practical objections. They may not be adequately trained theologically. The congregation may not be willing to have laymen preach. Questions of personality enter in. A particular layman, since he has not the accepted hierarchical status of the ordained priest, may not be acceptable to any given congregation, not because of any theological objection, but because his standing will have to depend on personal and individual factors which may or may not be accepted by the congregation as a whole. The difficulty would remain even if he were given a specific charge by the bishop. People are able to accept a dull or even domineering cleric. After all, they think, he is a priest, and boring priests have to be put up with. But a boring layman is something else, or a layman with whom one is having a business quarrel or a family quarrel. No doubt spiritual maturity could overcome these handicaps, but the practical problems are there. Laymen in fact have taken on many tasks in the missions and in areas where there is a shortage of priests, or even no priest for Mass. But even here the evolution is towards a married diaconate.

Discussion is something else. There is an air of unreality when one reads or hears of moves to encourage discussion in church during Mass and after the sermon. In principle one can hardly object, provided the area of discussion is suitably defined. Presumably, the matter itself of the gospel is not strictly for discussion in an assembly of Christians, and a legitimate preacher is entitled to insist on the obedience of faith. St Paul at Athens found himself involved in discussion and came away with a certain disillusionment. He thereafter decided his task was to proclaim Christ crucified. Such a message limits the area of discussion. However, some feed-back from the congregation is, after all, as in any teaching situation, a normal device, indeed an essential one in some form or other. There has to be a meeting of minds. The speaker should know what is going on in the heads of those he is addressing. It is generally neglected. Priests would no doubt radically alter their style of preaching if they regularly received reports on what their congregation thought about their sermon. But again it may be questioned if this is a practicable proposition for the ordinary Sunday Mass situation. Small select groups may more easily function in this way. In the ordinary parish situation there is, as often as not, the simple question of time, and people may legitimately feel that discussion should take place on some other occasion.

The problem of time is indeed a great stumbling-block for any attempt at liturgical renewal. One runs up against it constantly. Keep it short, they say. Leave out the sermon. Don't hold up the celebrant. Sing one verse only of the hymn (No wonder we don't know any, and find it extremely difficult to learn new ones). Time counts. The people have to get home to mind the dinner, or feed the baby, or let mother come to the next Mass. We have to get the church aired, or cooled, or cleared up. People have to go away for the day, or get to the golf-course. In schools, we have to get the hall ready for school dinners, or get them back into the classroom. Anything, except give time to meditation on the word of God. Hence, vast areas of ignorance, a liturgical desert, spiritual immaturity, a slow and creeping take-over by superstitious and magical elements, loss of faith. If people have to go away early, they should be able to do so with an easy and adult conscience. We should not paralyse, bind and tie the service of the word of God because we are preoccupied with the clock.

People find a service long because they are bored. It is not that the liturgy takes too long. Time is a relative factor, depending on psychological states. The liturgy may be felt to be long because people are not fully en-

73

gaged in it. It has not been made meaningful and fruitful for them. It has not been effectively preached. Many (including priests) simply want to get it over and done with as quickly as possible. Like medicine, or the dentist. With this sort of tradition, it is unlikely that more sophisticated forms of lay participation in the form of discussion will ever find an easy entry.

At some stage, however, and in some way, the priest must listen to the laity, even in matters of faith. The functioning of the community is not confined to the liturgical assembly, even though that assembly has special properties. In practice, and for the time being, too many difficulties may be found in the way of the laity speaking in church (Canon 1342, section 2 is itself a difficulty), but that does not mean that the preaching of the priest or bishop should not be fertilized and enriched by proper consultation with the laity. The Council is clear that this is broadly necessary, and its influence must therefore be brought to bear on what the priest or bishop says in the name of the Church:

Priests must sincerely acknowledge and promote the dignity of the laity and the role which is proper to them in the mission of the Church... They should listen to the laity, consider their wishes in a fraternal spirit, and recognize their experience and competence in the different areas of human activity, so that together with them they will be able to read the signs of the times (*Ministry of Priests*, n. 9).

A major part of preaching should be this very reading of the signs of the times, the application of the light of faith to the concrete situations, social, political, moral, in which we find ourselves. If preaching is to be relevant and practical, it must achieve this kind of enlightened judgment, and for this, real co-operation with the laity is essential.

The teaching of the Council on the charismatic gifts would also seem to demand dialogue of this kind. The Spirit works in the Church not only through the gifts attached to the hierarchy of offices in the Church, but also by special gifts given to individuals, called 'charisms' or individual graces given for the good of the Church:

It is not only through the sacraments and the Church ministries that the same Holy Spirit sanctifies and leads the People of God and enriches it with virtues. Allotting his gifts to 'everyone according as he will' (1 Cor 12.11), he distributes special graces among the faithful of every rank (*The Church*, n. 12).

Individual members of the congregation may well have a special gift of prophecy or insight into the needs of the community. The gifts are given for the benefit of the community and not simply for the benefit of the individual. Should they not be able to communicate in some way with the assembly and let the Church enjoy the fruit of their special gifts, coming, as they do, from the Holy Spirit and given for the benefit of the Church?

Whilst the existence of these gifts is acknowledged, yet, precisely because they are individual, and because in any explicit affirmation about special gifts of God there is always a danger of delusion, the Council also stresses that these gifts are to be tested and tried, for they come under the authoritative scrutiny of the hierarchy, 'to whose competence it belongs, not indeed to extinguish the Spirit, but to test all things and hold fast to that which is good' (1 Thess 5.12, 19-21) (*The Church*, n. 12). That the Eucharistic assembly is the appropriate occasion for this testing and judging may well be open to question.

However we may settle the problem of dialogue between clergy and laity, and however we may manage to have the legitimate testimony and preaching voice of the laity heard even in church, we must at the same time maintain the reality of the hierarchical priesthood and the system of relationships based upon it.

For the priest at Mass is not merely a group-leader exercising a directive function like an equal among peers, even though he too, as an individual, must 'listen' to the word of God. His task is not merely, like a good discussion-leader, to 'decrease' in order that the interchange and cross-communication in the group may increase. In that situation, the man in the chair does well to keep out of it and not impose his authority. But it would be naive to transfer these categories without distinction to the liturgical assembly. Here are brought into operation the powers and relationships that derive, not from the sociologists' analysis of group-function, however much that analysis may have a contribution to make, but from the nature of the Church, and the specific differences in the shares in the priesthood of Christ that are exercised in the liturgy. To say this is not to say that there is no possibility of the lay voice being heard. In practice, in some cases, it may be a more effective voice. But in our thinking on the question, we must allow for the sacerdotal character, the authority of the source he uses in his preaching, and the hierarchical structure of the liturgical assembly, where each should perform his proper task:

In liturgical celebrations, whether as a minister or as one of the faithful, each person should perform his role by doing solely and totally what the nature of things and liturgical norms require of him (*Liturgy*, n. 28).

The laity receive their commission to preach from the Lord himself in baptism and confirmation. The whole People of God is a priestly and prophetic people and its tasks fall upon all according to their capacity and degree:

The laity derive the right and duty with respect to the apostolate from their union with Christ their Head. Incorporated into Christ's Mystical Body through baptism and strengthened by the power of the Holy Spirit through confirmation, they are assigned to the apostolate by the Lord himself (*Laity*, n. 3).

The Church's work is accomplished mainly through 'the ministry of the word and the sacraments', and these are 'entrusted in a special way to the clergy' (*ibid*. n. 6). But 'the laity too have their very important roles to play if they are to be "fellow-workers for the truth" (3 Jn 8). It is especially on this level that the apostolate of the laity and the pastoral ministry complement one another' (*ibid.*).

In other words, the laity have a function with regard to the ministry of the word. Their activity is a necessary complement to the work of the clergy. They are not mere delegates of the clergy, but, consecrated as they are and given a task by Christ himself, they have their own task to perform which is theirs by right of baptism and confirmation. It is 'proper' to them.

The principal way in which this is carried out is, of course, by the testimony of a good Christian life. But more is expected. They must be prepared 'to give an account, to those who ask, of that hope of eternal life that is in them' (1 Pet 3.15) (*The Church*, n. 10).

The voice of the laity has to be raised, not only in answer to questions from unbelievers, but also even to instruct and exhort the faithful themselves:

However, an apostolate of this kind does not consist only in the witness of one's way of life; a true apostle looks for opportunities to announce Christ by words addressed either to non-believers with a view to leading them to faith, or to believers with a view to instructing and strengthening them, and motivating them toward a more fervent life. 'For the love of Christ impells us' (2 Cor 5.14), and the words of the apostle should echo in every Christian heart: 'For woe to me if I do not preach the gospel' (1 Cor 9.16) (*Laity*, n. 6).

We need hardly look for a more explicit affirmation that the laity have a commission to preach the gospel. However, this task makes demands. The laity may not simply say what they like, no more than the priest. The preaching function consists in mediating the word of God. Therefore it requires familiarity with the sources of that word. We have heard, for example, many reactionary voices from the laity as well as clergy in the immediate post-conciliar era. Much of what is said is based on ignorance of the developing movements in the Church which the Council has ratified and confirmed. The mere fact that the laity speak does not endow their words with the authority of the gospel. 'Only by the light of faith and by meditation on the word of God can one always and everywhere recognize God... seek his will... make correct judgements...' (*The Church*, n. 4). Their speech will rely on their sense of faith, which in the light of the word of God can interpret events:

For by this sense of faith, which is aroused and sustained by the Spirit of truth, God's people accepts not the word of man but the very word of God (1 Thess 2.13). It clings without fail to the faith once delivered to the saints (Jude 3), penetrates it more deeply by accurate insights, and applies it more thoroughly to life. All this it does under the lead of the sacred teaching authority to which it loyally defers (*The Church*, n. 12).

If the laity are to be true preachers, then they too must become 'hearers of the word'. They must cultivate this faculty of the sense of faith by which they can learn discernment. It is not, for example, enough that they accept a 'doctrine' that they have learned by rote uncritically in early childhood, and carried unexamined into middle age. They must also have a right judgment, a capacity for penetrating the revealed word of God more deeply and applying it to changing situations. It is in this existential application that the specific role of the laity is to be found. This is their 'proper' role. In virtue of their close engagement with life they make judgments about the situations they live with in modern society. They then embody in their personal lives the word of God newly incarnate in and through them. On this is based in a special way their right and title to be heard by the clergy, bishops and priests, who in their turn can interpret and articulate the mind of the Church for those in need.

Chapter III of the *Decree on the Laity* lists the more important fields of lay action: church communities, the family, youth, the social milieu, national and international affairs. All provide a wide scope for the presentation of the word of God to the world. The active share women now have in our society is also mentioned as a reason for their assuming further responsibilities in the lay apostolate. The question of women as preachers is too large for us to consider in detail here, but of course, as teachers, catechists, writers, lecturers, they have always been active.

Perhaps the most important of all these fields is the family circle, wherein the word of God is first brought to birth:

Husband and wife find their proper vocation in being witnesses to one another and to their children of faith in Christ and love for him. The Christian family loudly proclaims both the present virtues of the kingdom of God and the hope of a blessed life to come. Thus by its example and witness it accuses the world of sin and enlightens those who seek the truth (*The Church*, n. 35). The family is, so to speak, the domestic Church. In it parents should, by their word and example, be the first preachers of the faith to their children (*The Church*, n. 11).

Here are the grass-roots of the ministry of the word. Without them, all else is weakened and endangered.

The text mentions co-operation with the Church communities as a field of the lay apostolate. In particular, any missionary and apostolic enterprises organized in the parish are commended to the support of all. This presupposes the modern sociology of the parish. It is not a closed group, concerned only with its own affairs. It has a mission to the world round about it. But further, if it is to be truly outgoing and to have a relevant community structure in this day and age, it has not to confine its vision to its own immediate locality. It must take account of the way modern society functions, how groups of people associate and have relationship, particularly in urban areas. It would be singularly outmoded for the modern parish to confine the activity of its members to the territorial limits of the parish boundaries.

However we define the structure of local communities, the tasks of the apostolate belong to these communities, of the diocesan community, as a whole. The work of evangelisation should appear as a community activity and actually be such. Apostolic parish activities in which the parish council has an effective and proper share would be one example. Another would be a group of catechists, lay or religious, working as a team in collaboration with the priests and complementing their work. In particular, we should have catechumenal groups: that is to say, a form of organization where prospective converts are introduced to the community at all levels, and not merely by way of the solo interview with priest or nun in the parlour (what the French call *'l'interview à tandem'*). These organizations, where they already function, are normally concerned with pagans coming to Christianity for the first time, but the technique may be adapted, particularly in its liturgical forms and structures, to the needs and mentality of the particular non-catholic Christians one is dealing with.

Catechumenal rites are mentioned both in the *Constitution on the Liturgy* and in the *Decree on the Missions*. The rite of baptism will take the form of several rites spaced out over a period of time, coming to a climax at Easter. As with all liturgy, the presence and witness of the community is vital. At present, the reception of converts can take on the appearance of a hole-in-corner affair in an empty Church. The reason is partly that they have not yet been introduced to the community. A developed liturgy along the lines mentioned would be of benefit, not only to the converts themselves, but also to the faithful who attend and take part.

Communal liturgy plays an important part in the process of training and introduction. The community, however, does not function only at these privileged assemblies. Socially, too, and in the many varied forms in which an effective catechesis may be given, the community should be active.

This Christian initiation through the catechumente should be taken care of not only by catechists and priests, but by the entire community of the faithful, especially the sponsors. Thus, right from the outset, the catechumens will feel they belong to the People of God (*The Missions*, n. 14).

As indicated here, we also need a more developed notion of the function of sponsors, or God-parents. They must be prepared to take on more responsibility in this properly lay function, both in the course of training, and in the follow-up after reception when the new convert needs further help. So often he is left to sink or swim. Many sink for lack of a helping hand.

CHAPTER IX

WHO PREACHES? II. THE BISHOP

Whilst there is no doubt that the laity share in the total mission of the People of God to preach the gospel, yet they do not have the powers that are given to bishops, priests and deacons in virtue of their consecration and ordination. At first this may sound strange. One would think that preaching, a form of speaking, is something anybody can do. They just have to say the right words. Also, it is evidently something anybody can do badly. Can we speak of some 'intrinsic power' given in ordination? Orders give a priest the power to say Mass, to forgive sins. That we can understand. Christ acts through the ministry of the priest and the rite of the Church. We are sure of that. But preaching would seem to presuppose so many qualities that are purely personal and individual, depending on what kind of man the preacher is. He may or may not be good with words, his education is a variable factor, his personality, his relationship with the people he is talking to – all these things and much more would seem to be far more relevant in conditioning and determining the scope and efficacy of preaching than the fact that he is an ordained priest.

There are two questions here: one of fact, and one of explanation. We can establish the fact easily enough; we can promise very little, and that only tentatively, about the explanation.

It is standard Catholic doctrine that members of the hierarchical priesthood receive according to their degree the power and commission, in a fundamental sense, to preach the gospel in virtue of their ordination. They also require a 'canonical mission', or explicit jurisdiction to preach, from the appropriate authority. An heretical preacher could be barred by his bishop. But when attempt is made to explain just how this power comes into operation, how it is conditioned by personal factors, how it is related to sacraments and their efficacy, then we enter an area where theology is still at this moment 'in progress'.

All preaching in the Church stems from the person of Christ himself and from his 'anointing' by the Spirit. The Church is the Body of Christ and the whole People share his priesthood, including the prophetic function of that priesthood. The bishops, especially insofar as their words and works reflect and express their unity with the Pope and the College of bishops, have the special consecration that enables them to act in the person of Christ, the Head of the Body, and so have a care of the community and a responsibility to the world outside. This care and responsibility they exercise when they faithfully preach. As a result of the special anointing of the Holy Spirit given them in their consecration (and to the priest or deacon in his ordination), the bishops can call upon the grace of God to help them in their ministry. It is this that ensures that the preaching ministry of bishop or priest has a share in the efficacy of the word of God in the Church in a way that is, generally speaking, more secure than the preaching voice of the layman.

To the Lord was given all power in heaven and on earth. As successors of the apostles, bishops receive from him the mission to teach all nations and to preach the gospel to every creature, so that all men may attain to salvation by faith, baptism and the fulfilment of the commandments (*The Church*, n. 24).

The text then goes on to deal in detail with this teaching and preaching office. Notice, however, that it is not simply a 'teaching' office. That word alone might suggest something dry, legal and academic, like the issuing of books of doctrines. The bishop is not merely a person who adds his *imprimatur* to a dry summary of theological propositions such as we used to find in the older catechisms. Indeed, his responsibility for providing a rule of faith remains. Teaching and preaching need guidance from official statements. But the bishop is not just an official censor. He is consecrated to provide leadership and edification, to build up the people in active faith, in union with the universal Church which he makes 'present' in his diocese. He has to herald the faith of the Church. He has to preach and proclaim it. Further, among his many powers and responsibilities, this preaching and teaching holds the highest priority:

Among the principal duties of bishops, the preaching of the gospel occupies a pre-eminent place. For bishops are preachers of the faith who lead new disciples to Christ. They are authentic teachers, that is teachers endowed with the authority of Christ, who preach to the people committed to them the faith they must believe and put into practice (*The Church*, n. 25).

All of this raises the question of priorities in the time and work of a bishop (and also, of his co-workers the priests). Modern dioceses are often very large and require a complex administrative structure. Great sums of money are involved. Bishops may find they have to spend so much time on various committees that they may comparatively rarely have opportunity to devote time and attention to preaching the gospel according to the contemporary mind of the Church in a practical and personal way. When they do emerge from the office, their utterance may sound outmoded and *passé*. It is not necessarily their fault, and it is too easy to comment at a distance. Bishops are frequently overworked. But, like the apostles, they have to face the problem mentioned in Acts: 'It is not right that we should give up the preaching of the word of God to serve tables' (Acts 6.2). The apostles solved their problem by appointing 'deacons', and presumably the answer therefore lies either in more delegation or more bishops. The question is a good example of the way in which an increased theological emphasis in the council (here on the ministry of the word) has become the occasion of radical thinking on very practical matters. It is the function of genuine pastoral theology to provide the guide-lines for practical arrangements and procedures in the exercise of pastoral responsibilities.

The teaching and preaching office can be exercised in many ways. A bishop may exercise it through the guidance and encouragement he gives to others. His authority lends powerful support to various enterprises, particularly those of an institutional nature such as catechetical and other pastoral centres.

They should also strive to use the various means at hand today for making Christian doctrine known: namely, first of all, preaching and catechetical instruction, which always holds pride of place, then the presentation of this doctrine in schools, academies, conferences and meetings of every kind, and finally its dissemination through public statements made on certain occasions and circulated by the press and various other media of communication, which should certainly be used to proclaim the gospel of Christ (*Bishops*, n. 13).

In the days after the Council of Trent, which itself emphasized the teaching and preaching office of bishops, the authoritative aspect of the office of bishops came to be stressed as a result of attacks, and perhaps to dominate our thinking about the hierarchy. Vatican II, whilst holding fast to the principle of hierarchy and authority, is careful to add that these responsible powers are a 'service' to the community of the People of God in imitation of the Master from whom they derive. This concept should have greater prominence now in our thinking about the 'ministry' of the word:

Now, that duty, which the Lord committed to the shepherds of his people, is a true service, and in sacred literature is significantly called 'diakonia' or ministry (Acts 1.17,25; 21.19; Rom 11.13; 1 Tim 1.12) (*The Church*, n. 24).

The concept is important. The more exalted the office, the more the individual is liable to indentify his own purely personal views, instincts, and attitudes with what he conceives the office itself to be and to demand from him. We have all known domineering clerics, whether they be religious superiors, parish priests, bishops, or the ordinary man in the pulpit. The trouble arises from a confusion of functional and personal relationships. A man does not have personal moral authority simply from the fact of holding office. In Christianity the only moral authority derives from the imitation of Christ who was meek and humble. The office of preaching is particularly vulnerable in this respect. It can only be preserved from abuse when there is a sense of 'objectivity', joined to a true 'service' of the word. That is one reason why the word 'proclaim' is so often used in regard to preaching. The preacher's basic function is not to say, 'Look at me', or 'I'm telling you', with the emphasis on the 'I', but, 'Here is what the Lord has done and said'. In performing that function he is acting for the good of the community. He points to the objective word of God as directed to the people, including himself. This should condition his style and manner of address. Not that he should water down the message, or cease to reprove the people for their faults. Quite the contrary. But it should appear that he is announcing not his own word, but the word of God. The words of the decree on the pastoral ministry of priests would apply to all preachers:

Priests must treat all with outstanding humanity, in imitation of the Lord. They should act towards men not as seeking their favour, but in accordance with the demands of Christian doctrine and life. They should teach and admonish men as dearly beloved sons, according to the word of the apostle: 'Be urgent in season, out of season; reprove, entreat, rebuke with all patience and teaching' (2 Tim 4.2) (*Ministry of Priests*, n. 6).

Here we have a balance between maintaining the correct respect for persons, yet at the same time insisting on the real exercise of the duty to preach, even when the message is unpalatable. This text also sets limits to the scope of mere discussion methods. In a functional, not a personal, sense the man in the pulpit, if he possesses a legitimate commission, is not on the same level as his audience. At the same time, he is there to 'serve'.

A further sign that the individual priest or bishop is not merely insisting on his own exaggerated personal views will be the extent to which it appears that he is in fact communicating the contemporary mind of the Church, and of the College of bishops as a whole.

The diocese is a kind of microcosm of the whole People of God. The pastoral preaching of the bishop renders operative something of the mystery of Christ present in the whole Church. His sacred powers are endowed with an objective power that is, to a certain extent, independent of his own personal qualities. His words will be imbued with power to the extent and in the measure that he acts in union with Christ present in the Church and reflects his mind:

A diocese is that portion of God's people which is entrusted to a bishop to be shepherded by him with the co-operation of his presbytery. Adhering thus to its pastor and gathered together by him in the Holy Spirit through the gospel and the Eucharist, this portion constitutes a particular church in which the one, holy, catholic, and apostolic Church of Christ is truly present and operative (*Bishops*, n. 11).

The unity and cohesion of this particular local community will be ensured, not by the arbitrary use of canonical power, nor by personal idiosyncrasy, but to the extent that the bishop is guided by the Holy Spirit and feeds his flock by the objective law of the gospel and the Eucharist. Then the Church of Christ may become effectively 'present and operative'.

CHAPTER X

WHO PREACHES? III. THE PRIEST

In the exercise of their pastoral care for the People of God, the bishops have the co-operation of the presbytery, the body of priests. In virtue of their ordination, priests share, in their degree, in the one priesthood of Christ. Deacons also participate in the preaching office, and the difference the sacrament of orders can make to them in the exercise of that office is explicitly stated in the *Decree on the Missions:*

For there are men who are actually carrying out the functions of the deacon's office, either by preaching the word of God as catechists, or by presiding over scattered Christian communities in the name of the pastor and the bishop, or by practising charity in social or relief work. It will be helpful to strengthen them by that imposition of hands which has come down from the apostles, and to bind them more closely to the altar. Thus they can carry out their ministrations more effectively because of the sacramental grace of the diaconate (*Missions*, n. 16).

The office of the priesthood is similarly conferred, along with its special powers,

by that special sacrament through which priests, by the anointing of the Holy Spirit, are marked with a special character and are so configured to Christ that they can act in the person of Christ the Head (*Ministry of Priests*, n. 2).

For the exercise of the office of Christ the Head and the Shepherd, 'spiritual power is conferred upon them for the upbuilding of the Church' (*ibid*. n. 6).

Bishops are to regard their priests as necessary co-operators, not merely in virtue of delegation, but in virtue of the fact that they are already ordained to this task and can call upon the assistance of the Holy Spirit:

Therefore, by reason of the gift of the Holy Spirit which is given to priests in sacred ordination, bishops should regard them as necessary helpers and counsellors in the ministry and in the task of teaching, sanctifying and nourishing the People of God (*ibid.* n. 7.)

In virtue of the sacrament of orders, priests of the New Testament exercise the most excellent and necessary office of father and teacher among the People of God and for them (*ibid.* n. 9).

In all of their ministries, priests act as co-operators with the bishop. Having received their fundamental designation at ordination, they remain dependent in the exercise of these powers, a dependence which is regulated by law. They are dependent, not only in the exercise of the power to say Mass (in the choice of where and when and for whom), or to forgive sins, but also in the exercise of the power to preach. Thus, the priest preaching, especially at the Eucharistic assembly, makes the bishop 'in some way present', and his preaching is an exercise of the special powers with which he was anointed in ordination.

The priest preaching acts in the name of Christ the Head. The layman does not so act. The phrase is used to underline the distinction between these powers and those of the common priesthood of the baptized and confirmed. Without this activity, the resources of the 'whole Christ' are not made present. Just as we cannot celebrate the Eucharist without an ordained priest, so too, without the priest, who renders the bishop present, the effective word of Christ in the Church is not made present in the fullest possible sense, though one allows for the extraordinary visitations of the Spirit through the special charismatic gifts.

The priest has a responsibility in regard to the community. One hears views propounded about changes in the way priests should live their lives today. It is sometimes said they should live externally as laymen do. Most of his tasks, it is said, a layman can do, but of course, we need a few ordained priests around who will 'offer the sacrifice'. No doubt the social patterns of a priest's life are open to change. But he should not be reduced to the status of the divine mechanic who can 'make sacraments'. This does not seem to reflect the teaching of the Council. The ordained priest has a care for the community as a whole, which he shares with his fellow-priests as a body, and with the bishop, the president of the community, with whom he co-operates and whom he renders present. He is 'father and teacher'; 'the ministerial priest, by the sacred power he enjoys, moulds and rules the priestly people' (*The Church*, n. 10). Much of this responsibility is connected with the fact that he is ordained to preach.

The argument, perhaps a little facile, could be put forward: the bishop's most important task is to teach and preach; the priest is a co-operator with the bishop; therefore, his most important task is to teach and preach.

The Council certainly says that preaching the word is his primary task *(primum officium)*:

The People of God finds its unity first of all through the word of the living God, which is quite properly sought from the lips of priests. Since no-one can be saved who has not first believed, priests, as co-workers with their bishops, have as their primary dùty the proclamation of the gospel of God to all. In this way they fulfil the Lord's command: 'Go into the whole world and preach the gospel to every creature' (Mk 16.15). Thus they establish and build up the People of God (*Ministry of Priests*, n. 4).

On the other hand, the Council also says that offering the Eucharistic sacrifice is his highest function. We need not enter into an argument about terms. The two are essentially related. All the ministries of the priest find their completion and perfect fulfilment in the Eucharist. All is ordered towards the solemn praise of the Church, and derives strength and power therefrom. But participation in the Eucharist makes demands, both on priest and people. The sacraments are sacraments of faith. It is the priest's task to ensure by his preaching, either at long range by his general pastoral work and liturgical catechesis, or more immediately within the context of a particular assembly, that the people are well-disposed. In this sense, his preaching function is primary and a *sine qua non*:

In the Christian community itself, especially among those who seem to understand or believe little of what they practise, the preaching of the word is necessary for the very administration of the sacraments. For these are sacraments of faith, and faith is born of the word and nourished by it (*Ministry of Priests*, n. 4).

The pulpit, of course, may not be the best place for many priests to perform their 'primary duty'. They may be ineffective in the pulpit, but first-class in the confessional, or at a sick-bed, or in visiting homes. Or they may offer the outstanding witness of a saintly life, which is the basic form of the expression of the word in the Church. But when he comes to say Mass, he is not a mere functionary performing a rite mechanically and saying a set form of words without any particularly conscious attempt to communicate with his congregation. He has to lead the community, by himself or through others, both inside and outside the church building, to a true interior and exterior devotion:

Pastors of souls must therefore realise that, when the liturgy is celebrated, more is required than the mere observance of the laws governing valid and licit celebration. It is their duty to ensure that the faithful take part knowingly, actively, and fruitfully (*Liturgy*, n. 11).

Fr Congar makes the point in this way:

Hence Christian worship consists, in the heart of its truth, in accepting gratefully this gift of God and in uniting to it that spiritual offering of our concrete existence. That is why priests are ordained not so much to 'say Mass' but in order to make the faithful commune in this worship of Jesus Christ, of which they celebrate the *anamnesis* (memorial) sacramentally... This demands more than ritual celebration (Yves M.-J. Congar, 'Sacramental Worship and Preaching,' *Concilium*, March 1968, p. 30).

For the priest to be effective in his life, his spirituality needs to be closely related to the exercise of his specifically sacerdotal pastoral ministries. Through them, his particular vocation finds its proper maturity. The task of preaching is primary. Perhaps the finest expression in the documents of the Council of the dignity of the ministry of the word, applicable in its way also to laymen, is to be found in the section on the spirituality of priests in the decree on their pastoral ministry, where it treats of the preaching ministry. The preacher, if he is faithful, co-operates, as an instrument with the work of Father, Son and Holy Spirit in the building-up of the People of God. It is a work of charity. Through Jesus Christ, the eternal Word, the testament of love is established. The preacher, in the commitment of his full freedom as a human person, joins himself, his mind, his will, his talents, to the mission of the eternal Word in the world. It is a 'ministry of reconciliation'. If he allows himself to be guided by the Spirit, he himself grows towards identity with the Word. Thus faithful, he is of service to the People.

Priests will attain sanctity in a manner proper to them if they exercise their offices sincerely and tirelessly in the Spirit of Christ.

Since they are ministers of God's word, they should every day read and listen to that word which they are required to teach to others. If they are at the same time preoccupied with welcoming this message into their own hearts, they will become ever more perfect disciples of the Lord...

As priests search for a better way to share with others the fruit of their own contemplation, they will win a deeper understanding of the 'unfathomable riches of Christ' (Eph 3.8) as well as the manifold wisdom of God. Remembering that it is the Lord who opens hearts and that sublime utterance comes not from themselves, but from God's power, in the very act of preaching his word they will be united more closely with Christ the Teacher and be led by his Spirit. Thus joined to Christ, they will share in God's love, whose mystery, hidden for ages, has been revealed in Christ (*Ministry of Priests*, n. 13).

SELECT BIBLIOGRAPHY

Bouyer, Louis: *The Word, Church and Sacraments in Protestantism and Catholicism* (Chapman, London, 1961)

Concilium: 'Preaching the Word of God', Volume 3, No. 4, March 1968 (Burns and Oates, London)

Davis, Charles: 'Theology of Preaching', in *Studies in Theology* (Sheed and Ward Stagbooks, London and New York, 1964, p.b.)

De Rosa, Peter, ed: *Introduction to Catechetics* (Chapman, London, 1968). Contains full bibliography on catechetics.

East Asian Study Week on Mission Catechetics (Bangkok): *Lumen Vitae,* 17, (1962) No. 4 (Brussels)

Grasso, Domenico: *Proclaiming God's Message* (University of Notre Dame Press, Notre Dame, Indiana, 1965)

Hitz, Paul: *To Preach the Gospel* (Sheed and Ward Stagbooks, London and New York, 1963, p.b.)

Jungmann, Josef A.: *The Good News Yesterday and Today,* ed. William A. Huesman (W. H. Sadlier, New York, 1962)

Milner, Paulinus, ed: *The Ministry of the Word* (Burns and Oates Compass Book, London, 1967)

Murphy-O'Connor, J.: *Paul on Preaching* (Sheed and Ward Stagbooks, London and New York, 1964, p.b.)

Nebreda, A. M.: 'Distinguishing the Different Stages in Missionary Preaching', in *Studia Missionalia,* 1962 (Gregorian University Press, Rome)

Rahner, Karl: 'The Word and the Eucharist', *Theological Investigations,* Volume IV, Chapter 10 (Darton, Longman and Todd, London, 1966, and Helicon Press, Baltimore)

Schmaus, Michael: *Preaching as a Saving Encounter* (Alba House, St Paul Publications, New York, 1966)

Semmelroth, Otto: *Parole Efficace* (Editions St Paul, Paris, 1963)

Symposium: *The Word,* compiled at the Canisianum, Innsbruck (P. J. Kenedy and Sons, New York, 1964)

INDEX